SWU-NAP- 012

UNIFORMS OF RUSSIAN ARMY DURING THE NAPOLEONIC WAR VOL.7

UNDER THE REIGN OF PAUL I
EMPEROR OF RUSSIA BETWEEN 1796 AND 1801
FLAGS AND STANDARDS

From the Viskovatov's greatest work:
"Historical description of the clothing and
arms of the Russian Army"

English translation by Mark Conrad

SOLDIER SHOP PUBLISHING

AUTHOR

Aleksandr Vasilevich Viskovatov born 22 April (4 May New Style) 1804, died 27 February (11 March) 1858 in St. Petersburg, Russian military historian. He graduated from the 1st Cadet Corps and served in the artillery, the hydrographic depot of the Naval Ministry, and then in the Department of Military Educational Institutions. He mainly studied historical artifacts and the histories of military units. Viskovatov's greatest work was the Historical Description of the Clothing and Arms of the Russian Army.

TRANSLATOR

Mark Conrad is an American historian with a great interest for all the Russian history.

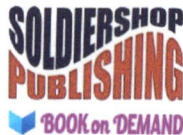

Title: **UNIFORMS OF RUSSIAN ARMY DURING THE NAPOLEONIC WAR VOL. 7 -**
Flags and Standards
By A.V.Viskovatov. English translation by Mark Conrad. First edition by Soldiershop.
Cover & Art Design: Luca S. Cristini. Plates re-colorations by Anna Cristini
ISBN code: 978-88-93270816

Published by Soldiershop publishing, via Padre Davide, 7 - 24050 Zanica (BG) ITALY. www.soldiershop.com

Publishing's notes

UNIFORMS
OF THE RUSSIAN
ARMY DURING THE
NAPOLEONIC WAR VOL.7

UNDER THE REIGN OF PAUL I EMPEROR OF
RUSSIA BETWEEN 1796 AND 1801

*

Flags & Standards

Saint Petersburg , 1800

HISTORICAL DESCRIPTION OF THE CLOTHING AND ARMS
OF THE RUSSIAN ARMY - A.V. VISKOVATOV
(First English translation by Mark Conrad)

Soldiershop is glad to presents the complete collection of the great job made by A.V. Viskovatov dedicated to the uniforms and weapons belonging to the Russian army during the Napoleonic period, until 1825. The time we considered corresponds to the reigns of two Tzars: Paul I, who reigned since 1769 until his murder on the 23rd of March 1801, and his son Aleksandr Pavlovi□ Romanov, that with the title of Alexander I, sat on the throne until the 1st December 1825.

Our reprint in based on the original 19th century volumes, to be precise the volumes from 7 to 9 are dedicated to the reign of Paul I; this first part is distributed on 7 volumes, having a numbering from 1 to 7. From number 10 to 18 of the original volumes, the second part is dedicated to the Russian troops under Alexander I. These still being worked on and they will be soon ready, distributed on twenty volumes approximately. Our new edition, the first ever published in English, both on paper and digital format, boasts a large number of color plates, many of them unpublished and coloured by our team of expert artists and scholars of uniformology. Each volume is based on 50/70 plates, always accompanied by the original translated text which describes the uniforms, the organization and the armament of the Russian army of the period.

A unique work in its genre, a must have in any respecting collection!

Aleksandr Vasilevich Viskovatov born 22 April (4 May New Style) 1804, died 27 February (11 March) 1858 in St. Petersburg, Russian military historian. He graduated from the 1st Cadet Corps and served in the artillery, the hydrographic depot of the Naval Ministry, and then in the Department of Military Educational Institutions.

He mainly studied historical artifacts and the histories of military units. Viskovatov's greatest work was the Historical Description of the Clothing and Arms of the Russian Army (Vols. 1-30, St. Petersburg, 1841-62; 2nd ed. Vols. 1-34, St. Petersburg - Novosibirsk - Leningrad, 1899-1948). This work is based on a great quantity of archival documents and contains four thousand colored illustrations.

Viskovatov was the author of Chronicles of the Russian Army (Books 1-20, St. Petersburg, 1834-42) and Chronicles of the Russian Imperial Army (Parts 1-7, St. Petersburg, 1852). He collected valuable material on the history of the Russian navy which went into A Short Overview of Russian Naval Campaigns and General Voyages to the End of the XVII Century (St. Petersburg, 1864; 2nd edition Moscow, 1946). Together with A.I. Mikhailovskii-Danilevskii he helped prepare and create the Military Gallery in the Winter Palace.

He wrote the historical military inscriptions for the walls of the Hall of St. George in the Great Palace of the Kremlin. (From the article in the Soviet Military Encyclopedia.)

CONTENTS

*

Preface pag. 5

*

Russian Army: Flags & Standards pag. 7

Insignia for Distinction pag. 29

*

Notes pag. 31

*

Plates pag. 41

RUSSIAN ARMY,
Flags and Standards, Insignia for Distinction 1796-1801

Contents

Changes in the uniforms and equipment of the Guards, Military Educational Establishments, Cossack and National forces, various separate commands, and military personnel not part of the Army, from 1796 to 1801:

Flags and Standards:

I. Grenadier, Musketeer, and Garrison Regiments
II. Cuirassier Regiments
III. Dragoon Regiments
IV. Guards
V. Military Educational Establishments
VI. Cossack Hosts
VII. National Troops
VIII. Senate Battalion

Insignia for Distinction

FLAGS AND STANDARDS *(Znamena i Shtandarty)*

I. In Grenadier, Musketeer, and Garrison regiments.

Until the ascension to the throne of EMPEROR PAUL I, *flags* and *standards* were treated along with accouterments and weaponry and had prescribed wear-out times. EMPEROR PAUL I decreed that flags as well as standards would serve indefinitely, and wherever he was present they were presented without any accompanying grant document (*gramota*), almost always from his own hands. In other troop locations beyond the IMPERIAL presence, flags and standards were supplied, except in a very few instances, with grant documentation signed by the EMPEROR.
All *flags* granted to *Grenadier*, *Musketeer*, and *Garrison regiments* throughout the years 1797, 1798 and 1799 were identical in pattern and dimensions, being made up of a *cross (krest)*, four *corners (ugly)*, and a *circle (krug)*. They were 56 inches (*2 arshina*) in both length and width, and made from silk, preferably *gros de Tours (grodetur)*. Sometimes camelot (*kamelot*) was used. The cloth of the flag was sewn to a wide piece of silk material called a "reserve" ("*zapas*"), which was

wound around the *pole* (*drevko*). It was then fastened along the seam by nails with gilded brass heads (Illus. 1224). At the bottom of the pole was fixed a gilded brass *base* (*podtok*). On the top was seated a similarly gilded brass flat *spearhead* (*kop'e*) with a *socket* (*trubka*). In the center of the spearhead was a gilt image of a two-headed eagle (Illus. 1225). Below the spearhead, at the edge of the socket, were hung two *tassels* of silver with black and orange silk, fastened to the ends of a doubled-over length of silver lace, exactly as prescribed for infantry officers' sword knots (Illus. 1225). The length of the pole was 10-1/2 feet (*4-1/2 arshina*); the spearhead, with socket—8-3/4 inches (*5-1/2 vershkov*); the length of each half of the lace ribbon, with tassel—28 inches (*1 arshin i 3 vershka*); height of the base—3-1/2 inches (*2 vershka*).

For each regiment, flags were issued in accordance with the number of Musketeer companies. The flag of the first—or honorary colonel's—company, invariably had a *white cross and colored corners*. On the flags for the remaining companies *crosses* were *colored*. For all flags the *circle* was light orange with a black two-headed eagle and—at the sides of the latter—green laurel wreathes bound with sky-blue ribbon. The shield on the eagle's breast was red, as in the Moscow coat of arms, while the edge around the shield, the chains of the Order of St. Andrew the First-Called, crowns, scepter, and orb were all gold (Illus. 1224). The *zapas* was made in the same color as the cross, and there were four colors possible for the pole: straw, white, coffee, and black [141].

The flags issued in 1797, 1798, and 1799 to *Grenadier*, *Musketeer*, and *Garrison regiments* were as follows:

Leib-Grenadiers – (in 1797) 10 flags: one with a white cross and sky-blue corners (Illus. 1224a); for the others a sky-blue cross and white corners (Illus. 1224b); straw colored poles [142].

Pavlovsk Grenadiers – (in 1797) 10 flags: one with a white cross and orange corners (Illus. 1226a); for the others an orange cross and white corners (Illus. 1226b); straw colored poles [143].

Yekaterinoslav Grenadiers – (in 1798) 10 flags: one with a white cross and corners half coffee and half dark blue, with a dark-blue (Illus. 1226c); for the others a coffee cross and corners half dark blue and half white (Illus. 1226d); yellow poles [144].

St.-Petersburg Grenadiers – (23 September 1798) 10 flags: one with a white cross and puce corners (Illus. 1226e); for the others a puce cross and corners half puce and half white (Illus. 1226f); white poles [145].

Astrakhan Grenadiers – (1798) 10 flags: one with a white cross and apricot corners (Illus. 1226g); for the others an apricot cross and white corners (Illus. 1226h); white poles [146].

Kiev Grenadiers – (30 October 1798) 10 flags: one with a white cross and puce corners (Illus. 1226i); for the others a dark-blue cross and corners half grey and half white (Illus. 1226f); white poles [147].

Moscow Grenadiers – (15 September 1798) 10 flags: one with a white cross and corners half dark blue and half light orange (Illus. 1226l); for the others a dark-blue cross and light-orange corners (Illus. 1226m); straw-colored poles [148].

Little Russia Grenadiers – (30 October 1798) 10 flags: one with a white cross and corners half rose and half black (Illus. 1227a); for the others a black cross and rose corners (Illus. 1227b); black poles [149].

Siberia Grenadiers – (15 November 1798) 10 flags: one with a white cross and corners half green and half black (Illus. 1227c); for the others a cross half green and half rose, with black corners (Illus. 1227d); white poles (150).

Phanagoria Grenadiers – (15 September 1798) 10 flags: one with a white cross and corners half rose and half green (Illus. 1227e); for the others a rose cross and green corners (Illus. 1227f); white poles (151).

Kherson Grenadiers – (15 November 1798) 10 flags: one with a white cross and corners half violet and half apple-green (Illus. 1227g); for the others a violet cross and apple-green corners (Illus. 1227h); black poles (152).

Taurica Grenadiers – (25 April 1798) 10 flags: one with a white cross and corners half yellow and half coffee (Illus. 1227i); for the others a cross half coffee and half yellow, with white corners (Illus. 1227k); straw-colored poles (153).

Caucasus Grenadiers – (21 January 1799) 10 flags: one with a white cross and corners half violet and half apricot (Illus. 1227l); for the others a violet cross and apricot corners (Illus. 1227m); white poles (154).

Belozersk Musketeers – (8 January 1798) 10 flags: one with a white cross and corners half sky-blue and half straw-colored (Illus. 1228a); for the others a sky-blue cross and straw-colored corners (Illus. 1228b); black poles (155).

Nasheburg Musketeers – (28 February 1797) 10 flags: one with a white cross and gray corners (Illus. 1228c); for the others a gray cross and white corners (Illus. 1228c); coffee-colored poles (156).

Chernigov Musketeers – (3 July 1798) 10 flags: one with a white cross and corners half celadon-green and half violet (Illus. 1228e); for the others a violet cross and celadon-green corners (Illus. 1228f); black poles (157).

New-Ingermanland Musketeers – (19 November 1798) 10 flags: one with a white cross and corners half straw colored and half dark puce (Illus. 1228g); for the others a cross half dark-puce and half straw-colored, with white corners (Illus. 1228h); coffee-colored poles (158).

Yaroslav Musketeers – (28 February 1797) 10 flags: one with a white cross and corners half raspberry and half black (Illus. 1228i); for the others a raspberry cross and corners half black and half white (Illus. 1228k); straw-colored poles (159).

Apsheron Musketeers – (30 July 1797) 10 flags: one with a white cross and corners half rose and half light sky-blue (Illus. 1228l); for the others a rose cross and light sky-blue corners (Illus. 1228m); black poles (160).

Smolensk Musketeers – (15 September 1798) 10 flags: one with a white cross and corners half mordoré (mordore– bronze-like reddish brown) and half green (Illus. 1228n); for the others a mordoré cross and green corners (Illus. 1228o); straw-colored poles (161).

Ryazhsk Musketeers – (20 November 1798) 10 flags: one with a white cross and green corners (Illus. 1228r); for the others a green cross and white corners (Illus. 1228q); black poles (162).

Kursk Musketeers – (15 September 1798) 10 flags: one with a white cross and corners half green and half puce (Illus. 1229a); for the others a dark-green cross and puce corners (Illus. 1229b); black poles (163).

Kozlov Musketeers – (7 December 1797) 10 flags: one with a white cross and corners half rose and half black (Illus. 1229c); for the others a rose cross and black corners (Illus. 1229d);

white poles (164).

Sevastopol Musketeers – (1 February 1799) 10 flags: one with a white cross and corners half sky-blue and half brown (Illus. 1229e); for the others a sky-blue cross and brown corners (Illus. 1229f); white poles (165).

Belev Musketeers – (1 February 1799) 10 flags: one with a white cross and corners half green and half rose (Illus. 1229g); for the others a green cross and rose corners (Illus. 1229h); coffee-colored poles (166).

Aleksopol Musketeers – (11 November 1799) 10 flags: one with a white cross and corners half brown and half rose (Illus. 1229i); for the others a cross half brown and half celadon-green, and rose corners (Illus. 1229k); black poles (167).

Schlüsselburg Musketeers – (3 May 1798) 10 flags: one with a white cross and corners half celadon-green and half rose (Illus. 1229l); for the others a rose cross and celadon-green corners (Illus. 1229m); black poles (168).

Bryansk Musketeers – (30 October 1798) 10 flags: one with a white cross and corners half yellow and half violet (Illus. 1229n); for the others a cross half white and half yellow, and violet corners (Illus. 1229o); coffee-colored poles (169).

Troitsk Musketeers – (1 February 1799) 10 flags: one with a white cross and corners half violet and half green (Illus. 1229p); for the others a violet cross and green corners (Illus. 1229q); straw-colored poles (170).

Ladoga Musketeers – (15 November 1798) 10 flags: one with a white cross and corners half dark brown and half celadon-green (Illus. 1230a); for the others a dark-brown cross and celadon-green corners (Illus. 1230b); black poles (171).

Polotsk Musketeers – (15 September 1798) 10 flags: one with a white cross and corners half dark brown and half rose (Illus. 1230c); for the others a dark-brown cross and rose corners (Illus. 1230d); black poles (172).

Archangel Musketeers – (15 September 1798) 10 flags: one with a white cross and corners half green and half brown (Illus. 1230e); for the others a green cross and brown corners (Illus. 1230f); black poles (173).

Old-Ingermanland Musketeers – (20 November 1797) 10 flags: one with a white cross and corners half rose and half light green (Illus. 1230g); for the others a cross half rose and half light green, and white corners (Illus. 1230h); white poles (174).

Novgorod Musketeers – (15 November 1798) 10 flags: one with a white cross and corners half dark brown and half sky-blue (Illus. 1230i); for the others a dark-brown cross and sky-blue corners (Illus. 1230k); white poles (175).

Nizhnii-Novgorod Musketeers – (15 November 1798) 10 flags: one with a white cross and corners half black and half celadon-green (Illus. 1230l); for the others a black cross and celadon-green corners (Illus. 1230m); coffee-colored poles (176).

Vitebsk Musketeers – (1 February 1799) 10 flags: one with a white cross and corners half rose and half dark blue (*sinii*) (Illus. 1230n); for the others a rose cross and dark-blue corners (Illus. 1230o); white poles (177).

Azov Musketeers – (15 November 1798) 10 flags: one with a white cross and corners half rose and half puce (Illus. 1230p); for the others a rose cross and puce corners (Illus. 1230q); straw-colored poles (178).

Orel Musketeers – (15 November 1798) 10 flags: one with a white cross and corners half puce and half apple-green (Illus. 1231a); for the others a puce cross and apple-green corners (Illus. 1231b); straw-colored poles (179).

Reval Musketeers – (23 September 1798) 10 flags: one with a white cross and corners half rose and half green (Illus. 1231c); for the others a green cross and rose corners (Illus. 1231d); white poles (180).

Tula Musketeers – (30 July 1797) 10 flags: one with a white cross and corners half puce and half light sky-blue (Illus. 1231e); for the others a puce cross and corners half light sky-blue and half white (Illus. 1231f); coffee-colored poles (181).

Yelets Musketeers – (6 September 1798) 10 flags: one with a white cross and corners half light green and half raspberry (Illus. 1231g); for the others a cross of three raspberry stripes and two light green, with white corners (Illus. 1231h); black poles (182).

Pskov Musketeers – (30 July 1797) 10 flags: one with a white cross and corners half green and half rose (Illus. 1231i); for the others a green cross and corners half rose and half white (Illus. 1231k); straw-colored poles (183).

Tambov Musketeers – (30 July 1797) 10 flags: one with a white cross and corners half very dark blue (*temnosinii*) and half puce (Illus. 1231l); for the others a cross of three white stripes and two very dark blue, with puce corners (Illus. 1231m); black poles (184).

Rostov Musketeers – (5 September 1798) 10 flags: one with a white cross and corners half light green and half black (Illus. 1231n); for the others a black cross and light-green corners (Illus. 1231o); coffee-colored poles (185).

Murom Musketeers – (30 July 1797) 10 flags: one with a white cross and corners half dark blue and half rose (Illus. 1231p); for the others a dark-blue cross and rose corners (Illus. 1231q); coffee-colored poles (186).

Staryi-Oskol Musketeers – (30 July 1797) 10 flags: one with a white cross and corners half light orange (*svetloaranzhevyi*) and half puce (Illus. 1232a); for the others a puce cross and light-orange corners (Illus. 1232b); white poles (187).

Tobolsk Musketeers – (2 July 1798) 10 flags: one with a white cross and corners half raspberry and half sky-blue (Illus. 1232c); for the others a raspberry cross and sky-blue corners (Illus. 1232d); white poles (188).

Tiflis Musketeers – (21 January 1799) 10 flags: one with a white cross and corners half puce and half siskin-green (*chizhovyi*– a delicate shade of yellowish green) (Illus. 1232e); for the others a puce cross and corners half siskin-green and half apricot (Illus. 1232f); black poles (189).

Voronezh Musketeers – (15 September 1798) 10 flags: one with a white cross and corners half dark puce and half very dark blue (Illus. 1232g); for the others a dark-puce cross and very dark blue corners (Illus. 1232h); white poles (190).

Kazan Musketeers – (21 January 1799) 10 flags: one with a white cross and corners half violet and half white (Illus. 1232i); for the others both cross and corners half straw and half violet (Illus. 1232k); straw-colored poles (191).

Moscow Musketeers – (30 October 1798) 10 flags: one with a white cross and corners half dark blue and half lilac (Illus. 1232l); for the others a dark-blue cross and lilac corners (Illus. 1232m); white poles (192).

Kabarda Musketeers – (21 January 1799) 10 flags: one with a white cross and corners half violet and half rose (Illus. 1232n); for the others a violet cross and rose corners (Illus. 1232o);

white poles (193).

Vladimir Musketeers – (15 November 1798) 10 flags: one with a white cross and corners half dark blue and half puce (Illus. 1232p); for the others a very dark-blue cross and corners half puce and half white (Illus. 1232q); white poles (194).

Uglich Musketeers – (30 October 1798) 10 flags: one with a white cross and corners half puce and half dark blue (Illus. 1233a); for the others a cross half dark blue and half white, and puce corners (Illus. 1233b); straw-colored poles (195).

Sevsk Musketeers – (13 August 1798) 10 flags: one with a white cross and corners half celadon-green and half violet (Illus. 1233c); for the others a cross half celadon-green and half violet, and white corners (Illus. 1233d); black poles (196).

Narva Musketeers – (30 October 1798) 10 flags: one with a white cross and corners half mordoré and half light sky-blue (Illus. 1233e); for the others a mordoré cross and light sky-blue corners (Illus. 1233f); white poles (197).

Dniepr Musketeers – (8 March 1798) 10 flags: one with a white cross and corners half yellow and half black (Illus. 1233g); for the others a yellow cross and corners half white and half black (Illus. 1233h); straw-colored poles (198).

Vyatka Musketeers – (27 October 1798) 10 flags: one with a white cross and corners half light sky-blue and half violet (Illus. 1233i); for the others a light sky-blue cross and violet corners (Illus. 1233k); coffee-colored poles (199).

Suzdal Musketeers – (21 January 1799) 10 flags: one with a white cross and puce corners (Illus. 1233l); for the others both cross and corners half puce and half violet (Illus. 1233m); straw-colored poles (200).

Kexholm Musketeers – (1 November 1797) 10 flags: one with a white cross and rose corners (Illus. 1233n); for the others a rose cross and white corners (Illus. 1233o); coffee-colored poles (201).

Viborg Musketeers – (5 April 1798) 10 flags: one with a white cross and corners half yellow and half puce (Illus. 1233p); for the others a puce cross and yellow corners (Illus. 1233q); coffee-colored poles (202).

Ryazan Musketeers – (21 August 1798) 10 flags: one with a white cross and raspberry corners (Illus. 1234a); for the others a raspberry cross and white corners (Illus. 1234b); white poles (203).

Neva Musketeers – (10 August 1798) 10 flags: one with a white cross and puce corners (Illus. 1234c); for the others a puce cross and white corners (Illus. 1234d); black poles (204).

Velikie-Luki Musketeers – (28 September 1797) 10 flags: one with a white cross and corners half straw-colored and half black (Illus. 1234e); for the others a straw-colored cross and black corners (Illus. 1234f); black poles (205).

Sofiya Musketeers – (31 August 1798) 10 flags: one with a white cross and corners half puce and half green (Illus. 1234g); for the others a cross half green and half puce, and white corners (Illus. 1234h); coffee-colored poles (206).

Shirvan Musketeers – (21 January 1799) 10 flags: one with a white cross and corners half gray (*dikii*) and half puce (Illus. 1234i); for the others a gray cross and puce corners (Illus. 1234k); white poles (207).

Perm Musketeers – (15 September 1798) 10 flags: one with a white cross and corners half light brown and half green (Illus. 1234l); for the others a light-brown cross and green corners (Illus. 1234m); white poles (208).

Nizovsk Musketeers – (15 September 1798) 10 flags: one with a white cross and corners half gray and half puce (Illus. 1234n); for the others a puce cross and gray corners (Illus. 1234o); white poles (209).

Butyrsk Musketeers – (5 July 1798) 10 flags: one with a white cross and corners half siskin-green and half puce (Illus. 1234p); for the others a cross half siskin-green and half puce, and corners half white and half puce (Illus. 1234q); black poles (210).

Ufa Musketeers – (9 January 1798) 10 flags: one with a white cross and dark-violet corners (Illus. 1235a); for the others a dark-violet cross and white corners (Illus. 1235b); black poles (211).

Rylsk Musketeers – (9 January 1795 (sic – should be 1798)) 10 flags: one with a white cross and corners half green and half very dark blue (Illus. 1235c); for the others a green cross and very dark-blue corners (Illus. 1235d); coffee-colored poles (212).

Yekaterinburg Musketeers – (9 January 1798) 10 flags: one with a white cross and corners half very dark blue and half puce (Illus. 1235e); for the others a very dark-blue cross and puce corners (Illus. 1235f); coffee-colored poles (213).

Selenginsk Musketeers – (21 January 1799) 10 flags: one with a white cross and corners half puce and half black (Illus. 1235g); for the others a puce cross and black corners (Illus. 1235h); black poles (214).

Tomsk Musketeers – (21 January 1799) 10 flags: one with a white cross and corners half puce and half green (Illus. 1235i); for the others a puce cross and green corners (Illus. 1235k); coffee-colored poles (215).

Arkharov's Musketeers – (18 December 1797) 10 flags: one with a white cross and corners half green and half pale pink (*blednorozovyi*) (Illus. 1235l); for the others a pale pink cross and green corners (Illus. 1235m); coffee-colored poles (216).

Pavlutskii's Musketeers – (22 February 1799) 10 flags: one with a white cross and corners half pink and half black (Illus. 1236a); for the others a black cross and on it a white cross, and pink corners (Illus. 1236b); straw-colored poles (217).

Leitner's Musketeers – (22 February 1799) 10 flags: one with a white cross and corners half pink and half green (Illus. 1236c); for the others a green cross with a white cross on it, and pink corners (Illus. 1236d); white poles (218).

Brant's Musketeers – (22 February 1799) 10 flags: one with a white cross and green corners (Illus. 1236e); for the others a green cross with a white cross on it, and white corners (Illus. 1236f); white poles (219).

Müller 1st's Musketeers – (22 February 1799) 10 flags: one with a white cross and violet (Illus. 1236g); for the others a violet cross with a white cross on it, and white corners (Illus. 1236h); white poles (220).

Marklovskii's Musketeers – (22 February 1799) 10 flags: one with a white cross and corners half dark green and half apricot (Illus. 1236i); for the others a dark-green cross with a white cross on it, and apricot corners (Illus. 1236k); white poles (221).

Berg's Musketeers – (22 February 1799) 10 flags: one with a white cross and corners half pink and half very dark blue (Illus. 1236l); for the others a pink cross with a white cross on it, and very dark-blue corners (Illus. 1236m); white poles (222).

St.-Peterburg Garrison – (21 December 1797) 10 flags: one with a white cross and puce corners (Illus. 1237a); for the others a cross of three dark-green and two white stripes, and puce corners (Illus. 1237b); coffee-colored poles (223).

Moscow Garrison – (28 February 1798) 40 flags: one with a white cross and dark-blue corners (Illus. 1237c); for the others a dark-blue cross and white corners (Illus. 1237d); white poles (224).

Viborg Garrison – (25 October 1798) 20 flags: one with a white cross and corners half pink and half black (Illus. 1237e); for the others a black cross and corners half pink and half green (Illus. 1237f); straw-colored poles (225).

Fredrikshamn Garrison – (5 September 1798) 10 flags: one with a white cross and corners half black and half green (Illus. 1237g); for the others a cross of three white and two green stripes, and black corners (Illus. 1237h); white poles (226).

Reval Garrison – (13 June 1798) 15 flags: one with a white cross and pink corners (Illus. 1237i); for the others a pink cross and white corners (Illus. 1237k); straw-colored poles (227).

Riga Garrison – (13 June 1798) 20 flags: one with a white cross and mordoré corners (Illus. 1237l); for the others a mordoré cross and white corners (Illus. 1237m); black poles (228).

Archangel Garrison – (12 August 1799) 10 flags: one with a white cross and corners half green and half pink (Illus. 1237n); for the others a green cross and pink corners (Illus. 1237o); black poles (229).

Kazan Garrison – (15 June 1798) 15 flags: one with a white cross and violet corners (Illus. 1237p); for the others a violet cross and white corners (Illus. 1237q); black poles (230).

Orenburg Garrison – (31 August 1798) 20 flags: one with a white cross and corners half green and half gray (Illus. 1238a); for the others a green cross and gray corners (Illus. 1238b); black poles (231).

Tobolsk Garrison – (16 June 1799) 15 flags: one with a white cross and corners half sapphire (*yakhontovyi*) and half pink (Illus. 1238c); for the others a sapphire cross and pink corners (Illus. 1238d); coffee-colored poles (232).

Smolensk Garrison – (12 August 1799) 10 flags: one with a white cross and corners half orange and half light sky-blue (Illus. 1238e); for the others a cross half orange and half white, and corners half light sky-blue and half black (Illus. 1238f); white poles (233).

Selenginsk Garrison – (16 June 1799) 10 flags: one with a white cross and violet corners (Illus. 1238g); for the others a violet cross and white corners (Illus. 1238h); straw-colored poles (234).

Kiev Garrison – (19 November 1798) 10 flags: one with a white cross and corners half mordoré and half black (Illus. 1238i); for the others a cross half mordoré and half black, and apricot corners (Illus. 1238k); straw-colored poles (235).

Taganrog Garrison – (11 May 1799) 10 flags: one with a white cross and corners half light-cherry (*svetlovishnevyi*) and half dark blue (Illus. 1238l); for the others a light-cherry cross and dark-blue corners (Illus. 1238m); straw-colored poles (236).

Baltic Garrison – (12 August 1799) 5 flags: one with a white cross and corners half mordoré and half green (Illus. 1238n); for the others a cross half green and half mordoré, and white corners (Illus. 1238o); coffee-colored poles (237).

Dünamünde Garrison – (12 August 1799) 5 flags: one with a white cross and corners half dark blue and half puce (Illus. 1238p); for the others a cross half puce and half dark blue, and white corners (Illus. 1238q); white poles (238).

Irkutsk Garrison – (16 June 1799) 10 flags: one with a white cross and corners half smoke-colored (*dymchatyi*) and half dark blue (Illus. 1239a); for the others a smoke-colored cross and dark-blue corners (Illus. 1239b); black poles (239).

Kronstadt Garrison – (10 September 1798) 20 flags: one with a white cross and corners half mordoré and half dark blue (Illus. 1239c); for the others a cross half mordoré and half dark blue, and white corners (Illus. 1239d); coffee-colored poles (240).

Narva Garrison – (13 June 1798) 10 flags: one with a white cross and corners half pink and half white (Illus. 1239e); for the others a cross half dark blue and half pink, and white corners (Illus. 1239f); white poles (241).

Yelisavetgrad Garrison – (19 November 1798) 15 flags: one with a white cross and corners half pink and half puce (Illus. 1239g); for the others a puce cross and pink corners (Illus. 1239h); white poles (242).

Dmitrii Garrison – (11 May 1799) 15 flags: one with a white cross and corners half raspberry and half sky-blue (Illus. 1239i); for the others a white cross on a raspberry cross, and sky-blue corners (Illus. 1239k); straw-colored poles (243).

Azov Garrison – (11 May 1799) 10 flags: one with a white cross and corners half mordoré and half pink (Illus. 1239l); for the others a cross half mordoré and half turquoise, and pink corners (Illus. 1239m); black poles (244).

Omsk Garrison – (16 June 1799) 10 flags: one with a white cross and corners half violet and half pink (Illus. 1239n); for the others a violet cross and pink corners (Illus. 1239o); white poles (245).

Astrakhan Garrison – (11 May 1799) 20 flags: one with a white cross and corners half orange and half black (Illus. 1239p); for the others a cross half orange and half white, and corners half black and half raspberry (Illus. 1239q); black poles (246).

Tsaritsyn Garrison – (11 May 1799) 10 flags: one with a white cross and corners half raspberry and half green (Illus. 1240a); for the others a white cross on a raspberry cross, and green corners (Illus. 1240b); white poles (247).

Kizlyar Garrison – (11 May 1799) 10 flags: one with a white cross and corners half orange and half green (Illus. 1240c); for the others a cross half orange and half white, and corners half green and half black (Illus. 1240d); black poles (248).

Schlüsselburg Garrison – (12 August 1799) 5 flags: one with a white cross and corners half dark-blue with double-faced lilac material (*lilovyi, dvulichnoi materii*) and half black (Illus. 1240e); for the others a dark- dark-blue cross with double-faced lilac material, and black corners (Illus. 1240f); white poles (249).

Villmanstrand Garrison – (25 October 1798) 5 flags: one with a white cross and corners half very dark blue and half light brown (Illus. 1240g); for the others a cross half light brown and half dark blue, and white corners (Illus. 1240h); white poles (250).

Kexholm Garrison – (25 October 1798) 5 flags: one with a white cross and corners half black and half pink (Illus. 1240i); for the others a cross of three black stripes and two light sky-blue stripes, and pink corners (Illus. 1240k); coffee-colored poles (251).

Nyslott Garrison – (25 October 1798) 5 flags: one with a white cross and corners half light sky-blue and half mordoré (Illus. 1240l); for the others a cross half mordoré and half light sky-blue, and white corners (Illus. 1240m); straw-colored poles (252).

Arensburg Garrison – (12 August 1799) 5 flags: one with a white cross and corners half dark blue and half violet (Illus. 1240n); for the others a cross half dark blue and half violet, and white corners (Illus. 1240o); black poles (253).

Pernau Garrison – (12 August 1799) 5 flags: one with a white cross and corners half sky-blue and half pink (Illus. 1240p); for the others a cross half pink and half sky-blue, and white corners (Illus. 1240q); straw-colored poles (254).

Bakhmut Garrison – (12 August 1799) 5 flags: one with a white cross and corners half smoke-colored and half green (Illus. 1241a); for the others a smoke-colored cross and green corners (Illus. 1241b); straw-colored poles (255).

Tambov Garrison – (22 April 1799) 5 flags: one with a white cross and mordoré corners (Illus. 1241c); for the others a mordoré cross and white corners (Illus. 1241d); straw-colored poles (256).

Voronezh Garrison – (19 July 1798) 5 flags: one with a white cross and dark-blue corners (Illus. 1241e); for the others a dark-blue cross and white corners (Illus. 1241f); straw-colored poles (257).

Vladimir Garrison – (13 June 1798) 5 flags: one with a white cross and apricot corners (Illus. 1241g); for the others an apricot cross and white corners (Illus. 1241h); coffee-colored poles (258).

Simbirsk Garrison – (11 May 1799) 5 flags: one with a white cross and corners half black and half brown (Illus. 1241i); for the others a cross half brown and half black, and white corners (Illus. 1241k); black poles (259).

Nizhnii-Novgorod Garrison – (during 1797) 5 flags: one with a white cross and corners half green and half black (Illus. 1241l); for the others a green cross and black corners (Illus. 1241m); white poles (260).

Novgorod Garrison – (4 May 1798) 5 flags: one with a white cross and pink corners (Illus. 1241n); for the others a pink cross and white corners (Illus. 1241o); white poles (261).

Tver Garrison – (7 December 1797) 5 flags: one with a white cross and corners half violet and half straw-colored (Illus. 1241p); for the others cross and corners are half violet and half straw-colored (Illus. 1241q); black poles (262).

Aleksandrovsk Garrison – (12 August 1799) 5 flags: one with a white cross and corners half apricot and half dark blue (Illus. 1242a); for the others an apricot cross and dark-blue corners (Illus. 1242b); black poles (263).

Sudak Garrison (formerly Kirilov)– (12 August 1799) 5 flags: one with a white cross and corners half violet and half gray (Illus. 1242c); for the others a violet cross and gray corners (Illus. 1242d); white poles (264).

Petrovsk Garrison – (12 August 1799) 5 flags: one with a white cross and corners half dark blue and half white (Illus. 1242e); for the others a cross half dark blue and half celadon-green, and white corners (Illus. 1242f); black poles (265).

Balaklava Garrison (formerly Nikitinsk, and from 3 September 1799 assigned to the Corfu fortress – (12 August 1799) 5 flags: one with a white cross and corners half sky-blue and half puce

(Illus. 1242g); for the others an cross half dark-blue and half black, and puce corners (Illus. 1242h); straw-colored poles (266).

Perekop Garrison – (12 August 1799) 5 flags: one with a white cross and corners half dark blue and half smoke-colored (Illus. 1242i); for the others a dark-blue cross and smoke-colored corners (Illus. 1242k); black poles (267).

Stavropol Garrison – (12 August 1799) 5 flags: one with a white cross and corners half black and half sky-blue (Illus. 1242l); for the others a black cross and sky-blue corners (Illus. 1242m); coffee-colored poles (268).

Orsk Garrison (formerly Ozernaya) – (12 August 1799) 5 flags: one with a white cross and corners half dark green and half smoke-colored (Illus. 1242n); for the others an dark-green cross and smoke-colored corners (Illus. 1242o); straw-colored poles (269).

Kizilsk Garrison – (12 August 1799) 5 flags: one with a white cross and green corners (Illus. 1242p); for the others an green cross and white corners (Illus. 1242q); white poles (270).

Verkhneuralsk Garrison – (12 August 1799) 5 flags: one with a white cross and corners half cherry and half green (Illus. 1243a); for the others a cherry cross and green corners (Illus. 1243b); white poles (271).

Troitsk Garrison – (12 August 1799) 5 flags: one with a white cross and corners half light sky-blue and half brown (Illus. 1243c); for the others a light sky-blue cross and brown corners (Illus. 1243d); white poles (272).

Zverinogolovsk Garrison – (12 August 1799) 5 flags: one with a white cross and corners half dark brown and half celadon-green (Illus. 1243e); for the others a dark-brown cross and celadon-green corners (Illus. 1243f); straw-colored poles (273).

Pskov Garrison (formerly Senno)– (12 August 1799) 5 flags: one with a white cross and corners half puce and half sky-blue (Illus. 1243g); for the others a cross of three puce stripes and two light sky-blue stripes, and orange corners (Illus. 1243h); black poles (274).

Dünaburg Garrison – (12 August 1799) 5 flags: one with a white cross and corners half pink and half green (Illus. 1243i); for the others a white cross on a cross that is half green and half pink, and white corners (Illus. 1243k); straw-colored poles (275).

Vitebsk Garrison – (12 August 1799) 5 flags: one with a white cross and corners half sky-blue and half pink (Illus. 1243l); for the others a cross half sky-blue and half pink, and dark-blue corners (Illus. 1243m); straw-colored poles (276).

Polotsk Garrison – (25 October 1798) 5 flags: one with a white cross and corners half dark blue and half pink (Illus. 1243n); for the others a cross half pink and half dark blue, and white corners (Illus. 1243o); white poles (277).

Rogachev Garrison (formerly Mogilev)– (12 August 1799) 5 flags: one with a white cross and corners half raspberry and half green (Illus. 1243p); for the others a white cross on a raspberry cross, and green corners (Illus. 1243q); white poles (278).

Staryi-Bykhov Garrison – (12 August 1799) 5 flags: one with a white cross and corners half orange and half sky-blue (Illus. 1244a); for the others a cross half orange and half white, and corners half sky-blue and half black (Illus. 1244b); black poles (279).

Tomsk Garrison – (16 June 1799) 5 flags: one with a white cross and corners half violet and half yellow (Illus. 1244c); for the others a violet cross and yellow corners (Illus. 1244d); coffee-colored poles (280).

Semipalatinsk Garrison – (16 June 1799) 5 flags: one with a white cross and corners half dark brown and half very dark blue (Illus. 1244e); for the others a dark-brown cross and very dark-blue corners (Illus. 1244f); black poles (281).

Biisk Garrison – (16 June 1799) 5 flags: one with a white cross and dark-brown corners that are half mordoré with turquoise (Illus. 1244g); for the others a dark-brown cross and corners that are mordoré with turquoise (Illus. 1244h); white poles (282).

Petropavlovsk Garrison – (16 June 1799) 5 flags: one with a white cross and corners half celadon-green and half dark-blue (Illus. 1244i); for the others a cross half celadon-green with mordoré, and corners dark blue with lilac (Illus. 1244k); straw-colored poles (283).

Mozdok Garrison – (11 May 1799) 5 flags: one with a white cross and corners half orange and half green (Illus. 1244l); for the others an orange cross and corners half green and half black (Illus. 1244m); black poles (284).

Saratov Garrison – (30 July 1798) 5 flags: one with a white cross and brown corners (Illus. 1245a); for the others a brown cross and white corners (Illus. 1245b); straw-colored poles (285).

Rochensalm Garrison – (9 January 1798) 15 flags: one with a white cross and corners half pink and half black (Illus. 1245c); for the others a cross of three pink stripes and two white stripes, and black corners (Illus. 1245d); coffee-colored poles (286).

Sevastopol Garrison – (10 January 1798) 10 flags: one with a white cross and corners half pink and half green (Illus. 1245e); for the others a cross of three pink stripes and two white stripes, and green corners (Illus. 1245f); white poles (287).

Nikolaev Garrison – (19 November 1798) 5 flags: one with a white cross and corners half smoke-colored and half violet (Illus. 1245g); for the others a smoke-colored cross and violet corners (Illus. 1245h); white poles (288).

Nizhne-Kamchatka Garrison – (16 June 1799) 5 flags: one with a white cross and corners half black and half raspberry (Illus. 1245i); for the others a black cross and raspberry corners (Illus. 1245k); white poles (289).

1800 – New pattern flags were established for Grenadier, Musketeer, and Garrison regiments. As before, they consisted of: *cross, corners,* EMPEROR PAUL I's monogram within laurels and under a crown, and a *circle*, also under a crown, surrounded by two laurel branches. Within the circle was the image of a two-headed eagle hurling thunderbolts , and over the eagle an inscription: one one side of the flag—*"S nami Bog" ("God is with us"),* and on the other—*"Blagodat'" ("Blessing")* (Illus. 1246). This circle was light orange on all flags without exception. The eagle was black; red flame under the eagle's talons; the crown entirely gold; sky-blue ribbons tying the laurels, and under the eagles; the spearhead on the pole had the IMPERIAL monogram in place of a two-headed eagle, of two Cyrillic P's crossed over each other, and the numeral I (Illus. 1246) [290].

The colors prescribed for the 1800-pattern flags were as follows:

a) *For regiments in the Livland, Smolensk, Lithuania, and Brest Inspectorates*—one flag with a white cross and corners half black and half red (Illus. 1246a); for the others—a black cross and red corners (Illus. 1246b); for all—silver laurels, thunderbolts, and monograms on the corners [291].

b) *For regiments in the Ukraine, Dniester, Crimea, and Caucasus Inspectorates*—one flag with a white cross and corners half yellow and half white (Illus. 1247a); for the others—a white cross on a yellow cross, and white corners (Illus. 1247b); for all—gold laurels, thunderbolts, and monograms on the corners [292].

c) *For regiments in the Finland Inspectorate*—one flag with a white cross and corners half of a lighter shade of dark blue (*svetlo-sinii*) and half black (Illus. 1247c); for the others—a lighter shade of dark-blue cross and black corners (Illus. 1247d); for all—gold laurels, thunderbolts, and monograms on the corners [293].

d) *For regiments in the Orenburg and Siberia Inspectorates*—one flag with a white cross and corners half green and half yellow (Illus. 1247e); for the others—a green cross and yellow corners (Illus. 1247f); for all—gold laurels, thunderbolts, and monograms on the corners [294].

e) *For regiments in the St.-Petersburg and Moscow Inspectorates*—one flag with a cross half white and half raspberry (sic – should be a white cross with corners half white and half raspberry? – M.C.) (Illus. 1247g); for the others—a white cross on a raspberry cross, and white corners (Illus. 1247f); for all—gold laurels, thunderbolts, and monograms on the corners [295].

Flags of these patterns were granted during 1800 to the following units:

a) In the Livland Inspectorate: (Illus. 1246a and 1246b): 30 March—10 to the *Taurica Grenadier Regiment* [296], and 26 December—20 to *Balashev's Garrison Regiment* (made up of the Reval and Pernau garrisons) [297].

b) In the Smolensk Inspectorate: (Illus. 1246a and 1246b): 6 March—10 to the *Moscow Grenadier Regiment* [298], and 5 August—20 to *Prince Ghica's Garrison Regiment* (made up of the Dünamünde, Smolensk, Vitebsk, and Mogilev garrisons) [299].

c) In the Lithuania Inspectorate: (Illus. 1246a and 1246b): 28 February—10 to the *Archangel Grenadier Regiment* [300].

d) In the Ukraine Inspectorate: (Illus. 1247a and 1247b): 17 March—10 to the *Smolensk Musketeer Regiment* [301], and 30 August—20 to *Masse's Garrison Regiment* (made up of the Kiev and Kherson garrisons) [302].

e) In the Crimea Inspectorate: (Illus. 1247a and 1247b): 26 December—20 to *Koshelev's Garrison Regiment* (made up of the Nikolaev, Perekop, and Sevastopol garrisons) [303].

f) In the Caucasus Inspectorate: (Illus. 1247a and 1247b): 17 December—10 to the *Kabarda Musketeer Regiment* [304]; 1 October—20 to *Ol'vintsev's Garrison Regiment* (made up of the Taganrog, Dimitrii, and Azov garrisons) [305]; also 1 October—20 to *Graf Lieven 3rd's Garrison Regiment* (made up of the Astrakhan, Tsaritsyn, and Simbirsk garrisons) [306].

g) In the Finland Inspectorate: (Illus. 1247c and 1247d): 21 June—20 to *Plutalov's Garrison Regiment* (made up of the Schlüsselburg, Villmanstrand, Kexholm, and Nyslott garrisons) [307]; 5 August—20 to *Prince Gorchakov 1st's Garrison Regiment* (made up of the Viborg and Fredrikshamn garrisons) [308]; 30 August—20 to *Bolotnikov's Garrison Regiment* (made up of the Rochensalm and Arensburg garrisons) [309].

h) In the Orenburg Inspectorate: (Illus. 1247e and 1247f): 16 June—20 to *Lebedev's Garrison Regiment* (made up of the Orenburg, Tambov and Voronezh garrisons) [310]; 21 July—20 to *Pushchin 1st's Garrison Regiment* (made up of the Kazan and Tobolsk garrisons) [311]; 21 July—20 to *Sendenhorst's Garrison Regiment* (made up of the Semipalatinsk, Petrovsk, Verkhneuralsk, and Troitsk garrisons) [312]; 21 July—to *Gogel' 1st's Garrison Regiment* (made up of the Saratov, Zverinogolovsk, and Kizilsk garrisons) [313].

i) In the Siberia Inspectorate: (Illus. 1247e and 1247f): 5 July—20 to *Leccano's Garrison Regiment* (made up of the Irkutsk and Selenginsk garrisons) [314]; 5 July—20 to *Retyunskii's Garrison Regiment* (made up of the Omsk, Zhelezinsk, Biisk, and Tomsk garrisons) [315].

k) In the St.-Petersburg Inspectorate: (Illus. 1247g and 1247h): 2 April—10 to the *Senate Regiment*; 26 May—20 to *Marklovskii 2nd's Garrison Regiment* (made up of the Narva, Novgorod, Pskov, and Tver garrisons) [316].

l) In the Moscow Inspectorate: (Illus. 1247g and 1247h): 16 June—20 to *Graf Lieven 1st's Garrison Regiment* (made up of the Archangel, Vladimir, and Nizhnii-Novgorod garrisons) [317].

Flags of the Taurica and Moscow Grenadier Regiments, as well as of the Archangel, Smolensk, and Kabarda Musketeer Regiments, differed from the others described above in having—above the eagle in the circle, in gold on a sky-blue field—inscriptions detailing distinguished services rendered by these regiments in battles with the enemy. These inscriptions were:

a) Taurica Regiment—*"Za vzyatie znamya v srazhenii protiv frantsuzov v Gollandii pod g. Bergenom 1799 goda"* ("For capturing a flag in battle against the French in Holland at Bergen in 1799") (Illus. 1248) [318].

b) Moscow Regiment—*"Za vzyatie znamya u frantsuzov pri Trebii i Nure 1799 goda"* ("For capturing a flag from the French at Trebia and the Nura 1799") [319].

c) Archangel Regiment—*"Za vzyatie Frantsuzskago znamya na gorakh Alpiiskikh"* ("For capturing a French flag in the Alps") [320].

d) Smolensk Regiment—*" Za vzyatie Frantsuzskago znamya na gorakh Alpiiskikh"* ("For capturing a French flag in the Alps") [321].

e) Kabarda Regiment—*"Za vzyatie u Avarskikh voisk znamya pri reki Iore, 7-go Noyabrya 1800"* ("For capturing a flag from the Avar forces at the Iora River, 7 November 1800") [322].

In the same year of **1800** flags were granted to *Baron Sprengporten's* and *Saken 1st's* Musketeer Regiments, designated to be formed, but no information has been preserved regarding exact patterns and in what numbers [323].

II. In Cuirassier regiments.

Standards (shtandarty) granted to Cuirassier regiments in 1797, 1798, and 1799, on the same basis and made of the same material as for the infantry flags described above, were rectangular and measured 37-3/4 inches (*10 vershkov*) wide, at the staff, and 45 inches (*12 vershkov*) long. In the middle of the cloth, in the lower corner nearest the staff, was an embroidered image of a two-headed eagle in ascent, and in the upper corner opposite was a cross giving off rays. On all four corners are monograms of EMPEROR PAUL I within laurels and under crowns. Along the sides, between the monograms, were embroidered edges and laurel leaves, and a fringe was sewn to the three edges not touching the pole (Illus. 1249). The *poles* of the standards were, as before, green with gold stripes. The *spearhead* was gilded and had a two-headed eagle; the *base* was gilt; silver *cords* and *tassels*, with black and orange silk; gold *embroidery* and *fringe*, or silver, as explained above; gold or silver *laurels* around the monograms, according to the color of the embroidery and fringe [324].

The standards in each Cuirassier regiment were five, according to the number of squadrons. Those given to the first or honorary colonels' (*shefskii*) squadrons were white with colored fields behind the monograms, these being the so-called *corners*, almost always the same color as that of the field for the remaining four standards (Illus. 1249).

The standards granted to Cuirassier regiments during EMPEROR PAUL I's reign were as follows:

HIS MAJESTY'S Leib-Cuirassiers – (25 June 1798) 5 standards: one with a white field and sky-blue corners (Illus. 1249a); the rest with a sky-blue field and white corners (Illus. 1249b); silver embroidery and fringe [325].

HER MAJESTY'S Leib-Cuirassiers – (25 June 1798) 5 standards: one with a white field and raspberry corners (Illus. 1250a); the rest with a raspberry field and sky-blue corners (Illus. 1250b); silver embroidery and fringe [326].

Military Order Cuirassiers – (23 September 1798) 5 standards: one with a white field and black corners (Illus. 1250c); the rest with a black field and white corners (Illus. 1250d); gold embroidery and fringe [327].

Yekaterinoslav Cuirassiers – (9 January 1798) 5 standards: one with a white field and sky-blue corners (Illus. 1250e); the rest with an orange field and sky-blue corners (Illus. 1250f); silver embroidery and fringe [328].

Kazan Cuirassiers – (23 September 1798) 5 standards: one with a white field and crimson corners (Illus. 1250g); the rest with a green field and crimson corners (Illus. 1250h); gold embroidery and fringe [329].

Ryazan Cuirassiers – (26 February 1798) 5 standards: one with a white field and sky-blue corners (Illus. 1250i); the rest with a sky-blue field and white corners (Illus. 1250k); gold embroidery and fringe [330].

Yamburg Cuirassiers – (26 February 1798) 5 standards: one with a white field and green corners (Illus. 1250l); the rest with a green field and white corners (Illus. 1250m); gold embroidery and fringe [331].

Glukhov Cuirassiers – (26 February 1798) 5 standards: one with a white field and coffee-colored corners (Illus. 1251a); the rest with a coffee-colored field and orange corners (Illus. 1251b); silver embroidery and fringe (332).

Kiev Cuirassiers – (23 September 1798) 5 standards: one with a white field and straw-colored corners (Illus. 1251c); the rest with a straw-colored field and violet corners (Illus. 1251d); silver embroidery and fringe (333).

Nezhin Cuirassiers – (25 February 1798) 5 standards: one with a white field and white corners (Illus. 1251e); the rest with puce field and white corners (Illus. 1251f); gold embroidery and fringe (334).

Sofiya Cuirassiers – (9 January 1798) 5 standards: one with a white field and sky-blue corners (Illus. 1251g); the rest with an orange field and sky-blue corners (Illus. 1251h); gold embroidery and fringe (335).

Starodub Cuirassiers – (23 September 1798) 5 standards: one with a white field and dark-green corners (Illus. 1251i); the rest with a dark-green field and white corners (Illus. 1251k); silver embroidery and fringe (336).

Chernigov Cuirassiers – (10 February 1798) 5 standards: one with a white field and puce corners (Illus. 1251l); the rest with a yellow field and puce corners (Illus. 1251m); silver embroidery and fringe (337).

Riga Cuirassiers – (23 September 1798) 5 standards: one with a white field and sky-blue corners (Illus. 1252a); the rest with a coffee-colored field and sky-blue corners (Illus. 1252b); gold embroidery and fringe (338).

Kharkov Cuirassiers – (11 February 1798) 5 standards: one with a white field and pink corners (Illus. 1252c); the rest with a pink field and puce corners (Illus. 1252d); silver embroidery and fringe (339).

Little-Russia Cuirassiers – (11 February 1798) 5 standards: one with a white field and violet corners (Illus. 1252e); the rest with a violet field and light-green corners (Illus. 1252f); gold embroidery and fringe (340).

Friderici's Cuirassiers – (19 July 1799) 5 standards: one with a white field and lilac corners (Illus. 1252g); the rest with a lilac field and orange corners (Illus. 1252h); gold embroidery and fringe (341).

Neplyuev's Cuirassiers – (19 July 1799) 5 standards: one with a white field and siskin-green corners (Illus. 1252i); the rest with a raspberry field and siskin-green corners (Illus. 1252k); silver embroidery and fringe (342).

Zorn's Cuirassiers – (19 July 1799) 5 standards: one with a white field and yellow corners (Illus. 1252l); the rest with a yellow field and red corners (Illus. 1252m); gold embroidery and fringe (343).

III. In Dragoon regiments.

Since 1797 Dragoon regiments began to receive *standards* in place of their previous flags. They measured 45 inches (*12 vershkov*) in both width and height, and were of a pattern like that for infantry flags but with the eagle and laurels embroidered rather than drawn, and with the addition of a fringe (Illus. 1253). Poles with all their fittings were the same as for cuirassier standards [344].

Standards were granted to Dragoon regiments according to the number of squadrons. In the first or honorary colonel's squadron—with a white cross, and in the other squadrons—with a colored cross, as follows:

Vladimir Dragoons – (21 January 1799) 5 standards: one with a white cross and corners half pink and half sky-blue (Illus. 1253a); the rest with a pink cross and sky-blue corners (Illus. 1253b); gold fringe (345).

Astrakhan Dragoons – (7 December 1797) 5 standards: one with a white cross and corners half sky-blue and half straw-colored (Illus. 1254a); the rest with a straw-colored cross and sky-blue corners (Illus. 1254b); silver fringe (346).

Nizhnii-Novgorod Dragoons – (21 January 1799) 5 standards: one with a white cross and corners half orange and half black (Illus. 1254c); the rest with a white cross with three light-orange stripes, and black corners (Illus. 1254d); silver fringe (347).

Pskov Dragoons – (6 September 1798) 5 standards: one with a white cross and yellow corners (Illus. 1254e); the rest with a yellow cross and white corners (Illus. 1254f); gold fringe (348).

St.-Petersburg Dragoons – (26 March 1798) 5 standards: one with a white cross and celadon-green corners (Illus. 1254g); the rest with a celadon-green cross and white corners (Illus. 1254h); gold fringe (349).

Smolensk Dragoons – (25 August 1798) 5 standards: one with a white cross and corners half violet and half orange (Illus. 1254i); the rest with an orange cross and violet corners (Illus. 1254k); gold fringe (350).

Taganrog Dragoons – (21 January 1799) 5 standards: one with a white cross and corners half straw-colored and half crimson (Illus. 1254l); the rest with a crimson cross and straw-colored corners (Illus. 1254m); gold fringe (351).

Irkutsk Dragoons – (20 November 1797) 5 standards: one with a white cross and corners half sky-blue and half puce (Illus. 1255a); the rest with a sky-blue cross and puce corners (Illus. 1255b); gold fringe (352).

Orenburg Dragoons – (20 November 1797) 5 standards: one with a white cross and puce corners (Illus. 1255c); the rest with a puce cross and white corners (Illus. 1255d); gold fringe (353).

Siberia Dragoons – (20 November 1797) 5 standards: one with a white cross and corners half crimson and half celadon-green (Illus. 1255e); the rest with a crimson cross and celadon-green corners (Illus. 1255f); gold fringe (354).

Ingermanland Dragoons – (4 May 1798) 5 standards: one with a white cross and raspberry corners (Illus. 1255g); the rest with a raspberry cross and white corners (Illus. 1255h); gold fringe (355).

Narva Dragoons – (21 January 1799) 5 standards: one with a white cross and violet corners (Illus. 1255i); the rest with a violet cross and white corners (Illus. 1255k); silver fringe (356).

Rostov Dragoons – (3 May 1798) 5 standards: one with a white cross and dark-blue corners (Illus. 1255l); the rest with a dark-blue cross and white corners (Illus. 1255m); silver fringe (357).

Moscow Dragoons – (3 May 1798) 5 standards: one with a white cross and corners half orange and half sky-blue (Illus. 1256a); the rest with an orange cross and sky-blue corners (Illus.

1256b); silver fringe (358).

Seversk Dragoons – (26 February 1798) 5 standards: one with a white cross and corners half black and half orange (Illus. 1256c); the rest with an orange cross and black corners (Illus. 1256d); silver fringe (359).

Kargopol Dragoons – (25 June 1798) 5 standards: one with a white cross and sky-blue corners (Illus. 1256e); the rest with a sky-blue cross and white corners (Illus. 1256f); silver fringe (360).

Schreider's Dragoons – (19 July 1799) 5 standards: one with a white cross and corners half white and half dark-green (Illus. 1256g); the rest with a white cross on a dark-green cross, and white corners (Illus. 1256h); gold fringe (361).

Khastatov's Dragoons – (19 July 1799) 5 standards: one with a white cross and corners half very dark-blue and half puce (Illus. 1256i); the rest with awhite cross on a puce cross, and very dark-blue corners (Illus. 1256k); silver fringe (362).

In **1800** the ten-squadron Dragoon regiments of *Skalon*, *Pushkin*, and *Obrezkov*, formed from the Irkutsk, Siberia, Narva, Nizhnii-Novgorod, Vladimir, and Taganrog Dragoons Regiments, were each granted ten new standards: in the first squadrons—white with green corners, and in the other squadrons—green with white corners. In appearance and dimensions they were like cuirassier standards except with the inscriptions *"S nami Bog"* and *"Blagodat'"* in place of embroidery, and on the corners of the field as well as on the pole's spearhead—a double monogram, i.e. with two Cyrillic P's laid crosswise over each other. These monograms, and all embroidery and fringe in general, were gold (Illust. 1257) [363]. *Skalon's* regiment (from the Irkutsk and Siberia) received such standards on 26 May [364]; *Pushkin's* regiment (from the Narva and Nizhnii-Novgorod)—on 16 June [365]; and *Obrezkov's* (from the Vladimir and Taganrog)—on 22 June [366].

IV. In the Guards.

a) *In the Preobrazhenskii, Semenovskii, and Izmailovskii Regiments:*
EMPEROR PAUL I granted the regiments of Guards Infantry flags of the same size and pattern as for Army Infantry, but with some changes in the depicted images.

In **December 1796** the *Preobrazhenskii Regiment* received 15 flags, the *Semenovskii* 10, and the *Izmailovskii* 10. In the first companies these had white cross and in the other companies yellow crosses, always with corners the same color as the regiment's collars, i.e. in the first regiment— red (Illus. 1258a), in the second—sky-blue (Illus. 1258b), and in the third—green (Illus. 1258c). Gold crowns were in the corners of all these flags; along the edges between crowns—green laurel branches; in the middle, in a circle surrounded by laurel branches tied with a sky-blue ribbon—an image of a *Keizer-flag*, and above the circle, on a silver field—gold inscriptions, on one side *"Sim znameniem pobedishi"* (*"With this flag you shall conquer"*), and on the other *"Ne nam, ne nam, a imeni Tvoemu"* (*"Not for ourselves, but in Thy name"*). Poles were coffee-colored for all flags [367].

1798 January 2 – Flags were granted to the *Leib-battalions* of the above regiments. All had gold crowns on the corners, the same inscriptions as on the above flags, and the same circles and eagles as on the flags for Grenadier, Musketeer, and Garrison regiments in 1797, 1798, and 1799:

Leib-Battalion of the Preobrazhenskii Regiment—5 flags; one with a white cross and puce corners (Illus. 1259a); four with a puce cross and white corners (Illus. 1260a); for all—coffee-colored poles [368].

Leib-Battalion of the Semenovskii Regiment—5 flags; one with a white cross and sky-blue corners (Illus. 1259b); four with a sky-blue cross and white corners (Illus. 1260b); for all—coffee-colored poles [369].

Leib-Battalion of the Izmailovskii Regiment—5 flags; one with a white cross and green corners (Illus. 1259c); four with a green cross and white corners (Illus. 1260c); for all—coffee-colored poles [370].

1798 December 16 – On this date, i.e. the day EMPEROR PAUL I assumed the title of Grand Master of the Order of St. John of Jerusalem, the white crosses of this order were sewn onto all the above guards flags [371].

1799 January 6 – To replace all the above flags from both 1796 and 1798, Guards infantry regiments received new ones with the same inscriptions, circles, eagles, and Maltese crosses as before, with the addition of a gold monograms in the corners and inscriptions *"Blagodat'"* (*"Blessed"*).

Preobrazhenskii Regiment—25 flags; one with a raspberry cross on a white cross, and white corners (Illus. 1261a); the rest with a white cross on a raspberry cross, and raspberry corners (Illus. 1262a); for all—coffee-colored poles; spearheads with a double monograms [372].

Semenovskii Regiment—15 flags; one with a sky-blue cross on a white cross, and white corners (Illus. 1261b); the rest with a white cross on a sky-blue cross, and white corners (Illus. 1262b); for all—black poles; spearheads with a double monograms [373].

Izmailovskii Regiment—15 flags; one with a green cross on a white cross, and green corners (Illus. 1261c); the rest with a white cross on a green cross, and white corners (Illus. 1262c); for all—white poles; spearheads with a double monograms [374].

In **1800**, when the Life-Guards Preobrazhenskii Regiment was reduced in size by one battalion, the number of flags in the regiment was reduced by five. In this same year new flags were granted to all three regiments of Guards Infantry, of the pattern established in 1800 for Army Infantry and Garrison regiments, except with double-monograms in the corners. In honorary colonels' companies, the cross on the flag was white, the corners half puce and half white (Illus. 1263a); in the other companies there was a white cross on a puce cross, and white corners (Illus. 1263b). Along with this the color of the poles was changed, and from this time they were: in the Leib-Battalion of the *Preobrazhenskii Regiment*—coffee-colored, in the other battalions of the regiment—straw-colored; in the *Semenovskii Regiment*—black; in the *Izmailovskii Regiment*—white [375].

b) *In the Cavalier Guards Corps and Regiment:*
The Cavalier Guards squadrons formed in **1797** and disbanded in that same year did not have standards.

The *Cavalier Guards Corps* established in **1799** was granted at its very beginning elongated rectangular standards of raspberry material (*stoff*) with a white cross in the center and silver fringe. The standard was attached to the black horizontal bar with gilt clamps at its ends. The flat side of the clamps was decorated with a cross of St. John of Jerusalem (Illus. 1264a). This crossbar was held at its two ends by a silver cord intermixed with gold & black and orange & raspberry silk. The cord was passed through the standard's center pole on which instead of a spearhead was a white cross of St. John of Jerusalem resting on a gold ball [376].

Soon after the *Cavalier Guards Regiment* was formed, in the first half of **1800**, three puce standards with black corners and a white Maltese cross were granted. These had gold edges and fringes (Illus. 1264b). Within the spearhead was a Maltese cross of white enamel in a gold frame [377]. In the same year of 1800, except at its close, these standards were replaced with three new ones fastened to a black horizontal pole on whose ends were silver clamps with rings. This cross piece hung from two silver chains going to the left beak and talons of a two-headed silver eagle resting on a silver ball at the top of the standard's upright pole (Illus. 1264c). The pattern, size, and colors of these standards are not known [378].

c) *For the Life-Guards Horse Regiment*, EMPEROR PAUL I granted Cuirassier-pattern standards three times:
1796 December – 5 standards; one with a white field and orange corners (Illus. 1265a); the rest with an orange field and dark-blue corners (Illus. 1265b); gold embroidery and fringe [379].
1798 – 10 standards with inscriptions: on one side—*"Sim znameniem pobedishi,"* and on the other—*"Ne nam, ne nam, a imeni Tvoemu."* One standard had a white field and raspberry corners (Illus. 1265c), and the rest had a raspberry and straw-colored corners (Illus. 1265d); gold inscriptions, embroidery, and fringe [380]. (Note: *"Ne nam, ne nam, a imeni Tvoemu"* is from Psalm 115, "Not to us, O Lord, not to us, but to your name." M.C.)
1799 – 10 standards with inscriptions: one one side—*"S nami Bog,"* and on the other—*"Blagodat'."* One standard had a white field and raspberry corners (Illus. 1265e), and the rest a raspberry field and straw-colored corners (Illus. 1265f); gold inscriptions, embroidery, and fringe [381].

d) *In the Leib-Cossack Regiment:*

1799 January 6 – The *Leib-Cossack Regiment* was granted two flags of an antiquated banner style (*v rode starinnykh praporov*) measuring: along the pole—17.5 inches (10 *vershkov*), length—54 1/4 inches (1 *arshin 15 vershkov*). One of these flags, in the first squadron, was white with a gold fringe and a raspberry cross emitting gold rays (Illus. 1265g). The other—in the second squadron—was raspberry with a silver fringe, white cross, and silver rays (Illus. 1265h). The poles for these flags, as well as their spearheads, cords, and tassels, were the same as for standards in Cuirassier and Dragoon regiments [382].
1799 June 6 – The regiment was granted a third standard similar to the second [383].

V. In Military Educational Establishments.

1798 November 2 – Four flags were granted to the *Army Cadet Corps (Sukhoputnyi Kadetskii Korpus)* that in appearance and size were like army flags, but with the addition in the corners of the corps coat of arms that had been established as early as 1732. It consisted of a gold scepter of Mercury crossed over a gold sword. On one flag the cross was white and the corners half puce and half straw-colored (Illus. 1266a); for three flags the cross was puce and the corners straw-colored (Illus. 1266b); for all the poles were coffee-colored [384].

VI. In Cossack Hosts.

1798 April 19 – Six flags were granted to the *Ural Host*, made of white cloth with images painted on both sides with oil paints: the Uncreated Savior, the Archangel Michael, St. Mercurius the Martyr, and St. John the Warrior. In the space between the images, like the shape of a cross and edged with sky-blue material, were sewn five gold stars and four gold monograms of EMPEROR PAUL I, under crowns. Between the edges of the cross and the images was a border of gold galloon with likewise gold inscriptions: *"Sim znameniem pobedishi"* (Illus. 1267). Around the whole flag was sewn, also in gold, a glazet brocade border with gold fringe along it on three sides. The pole, spearhead, cords, and tassels were exactly like those described above for regular cavalry standards [385].

1798 August 10 – Flags were granted to both *Chuguev regiments*. The pattern and size were as for the Leib-Cossacks but all with a red cross. In the *1st Regiment* one flag was white and nine sky-blue, with gold rays and fringe (Illus. 1268a and 1268b); in the *2nd Regiment* one flag was white and nine green, with silver rays and fringe (Illus. 1268c and 1268d) [386].

1799 January 4 – With his own hands EMPEROR PAUL I granted a flag to the *Leib-Ural Sotnia*, of the pattern of the flags received by the Life-Guards Preobrazhenskii Regiment on 6 January 1799, except without the inscription *"Blagodat',"* i.e. this flag had a white cross on a raspberry cross, and raspberry corners (Illus. 1268e) [387].

1800 February 15 – A flag was granted to the *Don Host*, made of white cloth with gold fringe on three sides. It had gold monograms of EMPEROR PAUL I in the corners, within laurel branches tied with sky-blue ribbons, and under two gold crowns: Russian and Maltese. On one side of the flag, in the center in a gold circle surrounded by gold laurel branches tied with a sky-blue ribbon that had gold edges, was a two-headed Russian eagle under an IMPERIAL crown (Illus. 1269). On the other side in a silver circle surrounded by gold laurel branches with a sky-blue ribbon was depicted a gold radiant cross (Illus. 1269). On each side of the flag, over the eagle and cross, on a black ribbon with silver edges, was inscribed in silver Cyrillic letters: *"Vernopoddannomu Voisku Donskomu za okazannyya zaslugi v prodolzhenie kampanii protiv frantsuzov 1799 goda"* ("To the loyally subject Don Host for services rendered in the continuation of the campaign against the French in the year 1799") [388].

VII. In National Forces.

1798 September 15 – The *Lithuanian-Tatar* and *Polish Horse Regiments* were each granted 10 flags like that for the Leib-Cossacks, with silver fringe. In the *Lithuanian-Tatar Regiment* one flag was white and nine sky-blue; all had gold eagles and radiant crosses as on standards for Cuirassier regiments (Illus. 1270a and 1270b). In the *Polish Regiment* one flag was white and nine puce; all had a crimson cross with gold radiation (Illus. 1270c and 1270d) [389].

1799 January 15 – Flags and standards were granted to the *Prince Condé's Corps.* The flags were like those granted to Russian infantry regiments in 1797, 1798, and 1799, except with gold lilies in the corners instead of monograms. The standards were patterned after those for Russian dragoons and also had gold lilies in the corners. In regard to colors, these flags and standards were as follows:

a) *Prince Condé's French Noble Regiment* - one flag with white cross and corners (Illus. 1271a); nine flags with a white cross on a black cross, and white corners (Illus. 1271b); coffee-colored poles [390].
b) *Duke de Bourbon's French Grenadier Regiment* - one flag with a white cross and orange corners (Illus. 1271c); nine flags with a white cross on an orange cross, and puce corners (Illus. 1271d); coffee-colored poles [391].
c) *Duke of Hohenlohe's German Regiment* - one flag with a white cross and black corners (Illus. 1271e); nine flags with a white cross on a black cross, and dark-blue corners (Illus. 12171f); coffee-colored poles [392].
d) *Duke de Berry's Noble Dragoon Regiment* - one standard with a white field and sky-blue corners (Illus. 1271g); four standards with a black field and sky-blue corners (Illus. 12171h); silver embroidery and fringe [393].
e) *Duke d'Enghien's Dragoon Regiment Regiment* - one standard with a white field and sky-blue corners (Illus. 1271i); four standards with a yellow field and sky-blue corners (Illus. 12171k); silver embroidery and fringe [394].

1800 February 16 – For distinction shown in battle with French republican forces *"at Constance"*, the *Duke de Bourbon's Grenadier Regiment* was granted new flags with an inscription explaining this honor, but the exact wording is unknown [395].

VIII. In the Senate Battalion.

1799 – The *Senate Battalion* was granted five flags of the pattern for all infantry flags of that time. One flag had a white cross and corners that were half orange and half black (Illus. 1272a); four flags had a cross half orange and half white, and corners half black and half raspberry (Illus. 1272b); black poles [396].
During the reign of EMPEROR PAUL I, flags were not received by: in the Guards—Life-Guards Jäger, Artillery, and Garrison battalions; in the Army—Jäger, Hussar, Artillery, and Pioneer regiments; among Military Educational establishments—2nd Cadet Corps, Shklov Cadet Corps, and IMPERIAL Military Orphans' Home; and from National troops—the Greek Balaclava Battalion. The only Cossack troops granted flags were those mentioned above, namely: Ural and Don Hosts, Leib-Ural Sotnia, and both Chuguev regiments.

INSIGNIA FOR DISTINCTION *(ZNAKI OTLICHII)*

1796 November 12 – For non-commissioned officers and privates who served 20 years without reproach, there was established the , being a gilded silver medal on whose face was a red cross inside a red rim and under a gold crown, and on whose reverse was again a red rim within which was inscribed the serial number of the award (Illus. 1273a). This insignia was prescribed to be worn in a coat's buttonhole on a red ribbon with yellow edges [397].

1798 February 5 – Silver trumpets and kettledrums awarded to regiments were ordered to be considered [398].

1800 October 10 – It was ordered that lower military ranks who had previously earned the St.-Anne medal were to be awarded , i.e. a brass cross with lilies in the corners and the serial number on the back (Illus. 1273b). This cross was worn in a buttonhole on a black ribbon [399].

During the reign of EMPEROR PAUL I the orders of St. George the Martyr and St. Vladimir 4th class with bow were not awarded, and military deeds by generals and field and company-grade officers were rewarded by the orders of St. Anne 1st, 2nd, and 3rd classes, and St. John of Jerusalem, which were also given for services by civil officials. The orders of St. Andrew the First-Called Apostle and St. Alexander Nevsky were reserved, as before, for higher general officers.

Distinctions established by EMPEROR PAUL I for military deeds not by individuals but by military units as a whole included: and or ( ).

that described a military feat were, as already related above, granted to the following units:

1800 February 15 – To the Don Host, with the inscription:

1800 February 16 – To the Duke de Bourbon's Grenadier Regiment for distinction "," but the exact words are unknown.

1800 February 28 – To the Archangel Musketeer Regiment, with the inscription "

1800 March 6 - To the Moscow Grenadier Regiment, with the inscription

1800 March 17 – To the Smolensk Musketeer Regiment, with the inscription

1800 March 30 – To the Taurica Grenadier Regiment, with the inscription

1800 December 17 – To the Kabarda Musketeer Regiment, with the inscription

On **16 July 1799**, the was awarded to the following regiments that served in Italy under the command of Generalissimus Prince Suvorov: , , , , , , and , and the and [400]. This distinction had been granted to two more Musketeer regiments, the and —to the first in **1797** for maneuvers carried out in the HIGHEST presence near the town of Narva [401], and to the second on **14 May 1798** for pacifying peasants at the village of Brasov in Orel Province in February of 1797 [402].

This enumeration of awards established and granted by EMPEROR PAUL I for the services and deeds of units as a whole and of individuals in particular brings an end to the 100-year period from the time EMPEROR PETER I definitely reformed Russia's military forces to EMPEROR ALEXANDER I's ascension to the throne. With the turn of the new, 19th, century, there began again a new epoch for the Russian Army.

Russian soldiers in ancient prints of 1796

NOTES

(141) There were no special rules for making flags, or at least none were found. Everything stated here about their dimensions and appearance is based on flags from the time of EMPERORPAUL I preserved up to now, in drawings as well as in actual items.

(142) *Chronicle of the Russian Army*, compiled by Prince Dolgorukov, No 8, and this same number in the drawings of flags and standards accompanying this Chronicle and located in HIS IMPERIAL MAJESTY's Own Library, catalogued under No 332.

(143) Ditto, No 9.

(144) Ditto, No 10.

(145) HIGHEST Grant (*gramota*) of 13 September 1798; *Chronicle of the Russian Imperial Army*, compiled by Prince Dolgorukov, No. 11, and this same number in the drawings cited above in Note 142.

(146) Ditto, No 12.

(147) HIGHEST Grant of 30 October 1798; *Chronicle of the Russian Imperial Army*, compiled by Prince Dolgorukov, No. 13, and this same number in the drawings cited above in Note 142.

(148) HIGHEST Grant of 15 September 1798; *Chronicle of the Russian Imperial Army*, compiled by Prince Dolgorukov, No. 14, and this same number in the drawings cited above in Note 142.

(149) HIGHEST Grant of 30 October 1798; *Chronicle of the Russian Imperial Army*, compiled by Prince Dolgorukov, No. 15, and this same number in the drawings cited above in Note 142.

(150) HIGHEST Grant of 15 November 1798; *Chronicle of the Russian Imperial Army*, compiled by Prince Dolgorukov, No. 16, and this same number in the drawings cited above in Note 142.

(151) HIGHEST Grant of 15 September 1798; *Chronicle of the Russian Imperial Army*, compiled by Prince Dolgorukov, No. 17, and this same number in the drawings cited above in Note 142.

(152) HIGHEST Grant of 15 November 1798; *Chronicle of the Russian Imperial Army*, compiled by Prince Dolgorukov, No. 18, and this same number in the drawings cited above in Note 142.

(153) HIGHEST Grant of 25 April 1798; *Chronicle of the Russian Imperial Army*, compiled by Prince Dolgorukov, No. 19, and this same number in the drawings cited above in Note 142.

(154) HIGHEST Grant of 21 January 1799; *Chronicle of the Russian Imperial Army*, compiled by Prince Dolgorukov, No. 20, and this same number in the drawings cited above in Note 142.

(155) Ditto, No 21.

(156) Ditto, No 22.

(157) HIGHEST Grant of 3 July 1798; *Chronicle of the Russian Imperial Army*, compiled by Prince Dolgorukov, No. 23, and this same number in the drawings cited above in Note 142.

(158) HIGHEST Grant of 19 November 1798; *Chronicle of the Russian Imperial Army*, compiled by Prince Dolgorukov, No. 24, and this same number in the drawings cited above in Note 142.

(159) *Chronicle of the Russian Imperial Army*, compiled by Prince Dolgorukov, No. 25, and this same number in the drawings cited above in Note 142.

(160) Ditto, No 26.

(161) HIGHEST Grant of 15 September 1798; *Chronicle of the Russian Imperial Army*, compiled by Prince Dolgorukov, No. 27, and this same number in the drawings cited above in Note 142.

(162) HIGHEST Grant of 20 November 1797; *Chronicle of the Russian Imperial Army*, compiled by Prince Dolgorukov, No. 28, and this same number in the drawings cited above in Note 142.

(163) HIGHEST Grant of 15 September 1798; *Chronicle of the Russian Imperial Army*, compiled by Prince Dolgorukov, No. 29, and this same number in the drawings cited above in Note 142.

(164) HIGHEST Grant of 7 December 1797; *Chronicle of the Russian Imperial Army*, compiled by Prince Dolgorukov, No. 30, and this same number in the drawings cited above in Note 142.

(165) HIGHEST Grant of 1 February 1799; *Chronicle of the Russian Imperial Army*, compiled by Prince Dolgorukov, No. 31, and this same number in the drawings cited above in Note 142.

(166) HIGHEST Grant of 1 February 1799; *Chronicle of the Russian Imperial Army*, compiled by Prince Dolgorukov, No. 32, and this same number in the drawings cited above in Note 142.

(167) HIGHEST Grant of 15 November 1798; *Chronicle of the Russian Imperial Army*, compiled by Prince Dolgorukov, No. 33, and this same number in the drawings cited above in Note 142.

(168) HIGHEST Grant of 3 May 1798; *Chronicle of the Russian Imperial Army*, compiled by Prince Dolgorukov, No. 34, and this same number in the drawings cited above in Note 142.

(169) HIGHEST Grant of 30 October 1798; *Chronicle of the Russian Imperial Army*, compiled by Prince Dolgorukov, No. 35, and this same number in the drawings cited above in Note 142.

(170) HIGHEST Grant of 1 February 1799; *Chronicle of the Russian Imperial Army*, compiled by Prince Dolgorukov, No. 36, and this same number in the drawings cited above in Note 142.

(171) HIGHEST Grant of 15 November 1798; *Chronicle of the Russian Imperial Army*, compiled by Prince Dolgorukov, No. 37, and this same number in the drawings cited above in Note 142.

(172) HIGHEST Grant of 15 September 1798; *Chronicle of the Russian Imperial Army*, compiled by Prince Dolgorukov, No. 38, and this same number in the drawings cited above in Note 142.

(173) HIGHEST Grant of 15 September 1798; *Chronicle of the Russian Imperial Army*, compiled by Prince Dolgorukov, No. 39, and this same number in the drawings cited above in Note 142.

(174) HIGHEST Grant of 20 November 1797; *Chronicle of the Russian Imperial Army*, compiled by Prince Dolgorukov, No. 40, and this same number in the drawings cited above in Note 142.

(175) HIGHEST Grant of 15 November 1798; *Chronicle of the Russian Imperial Army*, compiled by Prince Dolgorukov, No. 41, and this same number in the drawings cited above in Note 142.

(176) HIGHEST Grant of 15 November 1798; *Chronicle of the Russian Imperial Army*, compiled by Prince Dolgorukov, No. 42, and this same number in the drawings cited above in Note 142.

(177) HIGHEST Grant of 1 February 1799, No 113; *Chronicle of the Russian Imperial Army*, compiled by Prince Dolgorukov, No. 43, and this same number in the drawings cited above in Note 142.

(178) HIGHEST Grant of 15 November 1798; *Chronicle of the Russian Imperial Army*, compiled by Prince Dolgorukov, No. 44, and this same number in the drawings cited above in Note 142..

(179) HIGHEST Grant of 15 November 1798; *Chronicle of the Russian Imperial Army*, compiled by Prince Dolgorukov, No. 45, and this same number in the drawings cited above in Note 142.

(180) HIGHEST Grant of 30 September 1798; *Chronicle of the Russian Imperial Army*, compiled by Prince Dolgorukov, No. 46, and this same number in the drawings cited above in Note 142.

(181) Ditto, No 47.

(182) HIGHEST Grant of 6 September 1798; *Chronicle of the Russian Imperial Army*, compiled by Prince Dolgorukov, No. 48, and this same number in the drawings cited above in Note 142.

(183) *Chronicle of the Russian Imperial Army*, compiled by Prince Dolgorukov, No. 59, and this same number in the drawings cited above in Note 142.

(184) Ditto, No 50.

(185) HIGHEST Grant of 5 September 1798; *Chronicle of the Russian Imperial Army*, compiled by Prince Dolgorukov, No. 51, and this same number in the drawings cited above in Note 142.

(186) *Chronicle of the Russian Imperial Army*, compiled by Prince Dolgorukov, No. 52, and this same number in the drawings cited above in Note 142.

(187) Ditto, No 53.

(188) HIGHEST Grant of 2 July 1798; *Chronicle of the Russian Imperial Army*, compiled by Prince Dolgorukov, No. 54, and this same number in the drawings cited above in Note 142.

(189) HIGHEST Grant of 21 January 1799, No 63; *Chronicle of the Russian Imperial Army*, compiled by Prince Dolgorukov, No. 55, and this same number in the drawings cited above in Note 142.

(190) HIGHEST Grant of 15 September 1798; *Chronicle of the Russian Imperial Army*, compiled by Prince Dolgorukov, No. 56, and this same number in the drawings cited above in Note 142.

(191) HIGHEST Grant of 21 January 1799, No 64; *Chronicle of the Russian Imperial Army*, compiled by Prince Dolgorukov, No. 57, and this same number in the drawings cited above in Note 142.

(192) HIGHEST Grant of 30 October 1798; *Chronicle of the Russian Imperial Army*, compiled by Prince Dolgorukov, No. 58, and this same number in the drawings cited above in Note 142.

(193) HIGHEST Grant of 21 January 1799; *Chronicle of the Russian Imperial Army*, compiled by Prince Dolgorukov, No. 59, and this same number in the drawings cited above in Note 142.

(194) HIGHEST Grant of 15 November 1798; *Chronicle of the Russian Imperial Army*, compiled by Prince Dolgorukov, No. 60, and this same number in the drawings cited above in Note 142.

(195) HIGHEST Grant of 30 October 1798; *Chronicle of the Russian Imperial Army*, compiled by Prince Dolgorukov, No. 61, and this same number in the drawings cited above in Note 142.

(196) HIGHEST Grant of 13 August 1798; *Chronicle of the Russian Imperial Army*, compiled by Prince Dolgorukov, No. 62, and this same number in the drawings cited above in Note 142.

(197) HIGHEST Grant of 30 October 1798; *Chronicle of the Russian Imperial Army*, compiled by Prince Dolgorukov, No. 63, and this same number in the drawings cited above in Note 142.

(198) HIGHEST Grant of 8 March 1798; *Chronicle of the Russian Imperial Army*, compiled by Prince Dolgorukov, No. 64, and this same number in the drawings cited above in Note 142.

(199) *Chronicle of the Russian Imperial Army*, compiled by Prince Dolgorukov, No. 65, and this same number in the drawings cited above in Note 142.

(200) HIGHEST Grant of 21 January 1799; *Chronicle of the Russian Imperial Army*, compiled by Prince Dolgorukov, No. 68, and this same number in the drawings cited above in Note 142.

(201) *Chronicle of the Russian Imperial Army*, compiled by Prince Dolgorukov, No. 67, and this same number in the drawings cited above in Note 142.

(202) HIGHEST Grant of 5 April 1798; *Chronicle of the Russian Imperial Army*, compiled by Prince Dolgorukov, No. 69, and this same number in the drawings cited above in Note 142.

(203) HIGHEST Grant of 21 August 1798; *Chronicle of the Russian Imperial Army*, compiled by Prince Dolgorukov, No. 69, and this same number in the drawings cited above in Note 142.

(204) HIGHEST Grant of 10 August 1798; *Chronicle of the Russian Imperial Army*, compiled by Prince Dolgorukov, No. 70, and this same number in the drawings cited above in Note 142.

(205) *Chronicle of the Russian Imperial Army*, compiled by Prince Dolgorukov, No. 71, and this same number in the drawings cited above in Note 142.

(206) HIGHEST Grant of 31 August 1798; *Chronicle of the Russian Imperial Army*, compiled by Prince Dolgorukov, No. 72, and this same number in the drawings cited above in Note 142.

(207) HIGHEST Grant of 21 January 1799, No 65; *Chronicle of the Russian Imperial Army*, compiled by Prince Dolgorukov, No. 73, and this same number in the drawings cited above in Note 142.

(208) HIGHEST Grant of 15 September 1798; *Chronicle of the Russian Imperial Army*, compiled by Prince Dolgorukov, No. 74, and this same number in the drawings cited above in Note 142.

(209) HIGHEST Grant of 15 September 1798; *Chronicle of the Russian Imperial Army*, compiled by Prince Dolgorukov, No. 75, and this same number in the drawings cited above in Note 142.

(210) HIGHEST Grant of 5 July 1798; *Chronicle of the Russian Imperial Army*, compiled by Prince Dolgorukov, No. 76, and this same number in the drawings cited above in Note 142.

(211) HIGHEST Grant of 9 January 1798; *Chronicle of the Russian Imperial Army*, compiled by Prince Dolgorukov, No. 77, and this same number in the drawings cited above in Note 142.

(212) HIGHEST Grant of 9 January 1798; *Chronicle of the Russian Imperial Army*, compiled by Prince Dolgorukov, No. 78, and this same number in the drawings cited above in Note 142.

(213) HIGHEST Grant of 9 January 1798; *Chronicle of the Russian Imperial Army*, compiled by Prince Dolgorukov, No. 79, and this same number in the drawings cited above in Note 142.

(214) HIGHEST Grant of 21 January 1798, No 67; *Chronicle of the Russian Imperial Army*, compiled by Prince Dolgorukov, No. 80, and this same number in the drawings cited above in Note 142.

(215) HIGHEST Grant of 21 January 1799, No 66; *Chronicle of the Russian Imperial Army*, compiled by Prince Dolgorukov, No. 81, and this same number in the drawings cited above in Note 142.

(216) *Chronicle of the Russian Imperial Army*, compiled by Prince Dolgorukov, No. 82, and this same number in the drawings cited above in Note 142.

(217) HIGHEST Grant of 22 February 1799, No 165; *Chronicle of the Russian Imperial Army*, compiled by Prince Dolgorukov, No. 83, and this same number in the drawings cited above in Note 142.

(218) HIGHEST Grant of 22 February 1799, No 167; *Chronicle of the Russian Imperial Army*, compiled by Prince Dolgorukov, No. 84, and this same number in the drawings cited above in Note 142.

(219) HIGHEST Grant of 22 February 1799, No 170; *Chronicle of the Russian Imperial Army*, compiled by Prince Dolgorukov, No. 85, and this same number in the drawings cited above in Note 142.

(220) HIGHEST Grant of 22 February 1799, No 168; *Chronicle of the Russian Imperial Army*, compiled by Prince Dolgorukov, No. 86, and this same number in the drawings cited above in Note 142.

(221) HIGHEST Grant of 22 February 1799, No 166; *Chronicle of the Russian Imperial Army*, compiled by Prince Dolgorukov, No. 87, and this same number in the drawings cited above in Note 142.

(222) HIGHEST Grant of 22 February 1799, No 169; *Chronicle of the Russian Imperial Army*, compiled by Prince Dolgorukov, No. 88, and this same number in the drawings cited above in Note 142.

(223) *Chronicle of the Russian Imperial Army*, compiled by Prince Dolgorukov, No. 89, and this same number in the drawings cited above in Note 142.

(224) Ditto, No 94.

(225) HIGHEST Grant of 25 October 1798; *Chronicle of the Russian Imperial Army*, compiled by Prince Dolgorukov, No. 102, and this same number in the drawings cited above in Note 142.

(226) HIGHEST Grant of 5 September 1798; *Chronicle of the Russian Imperial Army*, compiled by Prince Dolgorukov, No. 103, and this same number in the drawings cited above in Note 142.

(227) HIGHEST Grant of 13 June 1798; *Chronicle of the Russian Imperial Army*, compiled by Prince Dolgorukov, No. 109, and this same number in the drawings cited above in Note 142.

(228) HIGHEST Grant of 13 June 1798; *Chronicle of the Russian Imperial Army*, compiled by Prince Dolgorukov, No. 108, and this same number in the drawings cited above in Note 142.

(229) HIGHEST Grant of 12 August 1799, No 967; *Chronicle of the Russian Imperial Army*, compiled by Prince Dolgorukov, No. 95, and this same number in the drawings cited above in Note 142.

(230) *Chronicle of the Russian Imperial Army*, compiled by Prince Dolgorukov, No. 138, and this same number in the drawings cited above in Note 142.

(231) HIGHEST Grant of 31 August 1798; *Chronicle of the Russian Imperial Army*, compiled by Prince Dolgorukov, No. 140, and this same number in the drawings cited above in Note 142.

(232) HIGHEST Grant of 16 June 1798, No 522; *Chronicle of the Russian Imperial Army*, compiled by Prince Dolgorukov, No. 154, and this same number in the drawings cited above in Note 142.

(233) HIGHEST Grant of 12 August 1799, No 973; *Chronicle of the Russian Imperial Army*, compiled by Prince Dolgorukov, No. 115, and this same number in the drawings cited above in Note 142.

(234) HIGHEST Grant of 16 June 1799, No 524; *Chronicle of the Russian Imperial Army*, compiled by Prince Dolgorukov, No. 148, and this same number in the drawings cited above in Note 142.

(235) HIGHEST Grant of 19 November 1798, No 524; *Chronicle of the Russian Imperial Army*, compiled by Prince Dolgorukov, No. 121, and this same number in the drawings cited above in Note 142.

(236) HIGHEST Grant of 11 May 1799, No 344; *Chronicle of the Russian Imperial Army*, compiled by Prince Dolgorukov, No. 135, and this same number in the drawings cited above in Note 142.

(237) HIGHEST Grant of 12 August 1799, No 524; *Chronicle of the Russian Imperial Army*, compiled by Prince Dolgorukov, No. 148, and this same number in the drawings cited above in Note 142.

(238) HIGHEST Grant of 12 August 1799, No 969; *Chronicle of the Russian Imperial Army*, compiled by Prince Dolgorukov, No. 111, and this same number in the drawings cited above in Note 142.

(239) HIGHEST Grant of 16 June 1799, No 525; *Chronicle of the Russian Imperial Army*, compiled by Prince Dolgorukov, No. 147, and this same number in the drawings cited above in Note 142.

(240) *Chronicle of the Russian Imperial Army*, compiled by Prince Dolgorukov, No. 90, and this same number in the drawings cited above in Note 142.

(241) HIGHEST Grant of 13 June 1798; *Chronicle of the Russian Imperial Army*, compiled by Prince Dolgorukov, No. 92, and this same number in the drawings cited above in Note 142.

(242) HIGHEST Grant of 19 November 1798; *Chronicle of the Russian Imperial Army*, compiled by Prince Dolgorukov, No. 122, and this same number in the drawings cited above in Note 142.

(243) HIGHEST Grant of 11 May 1799, No 347; *Chronicle of the Russian Imperial Army*, compiled by Prince Dolgorukov, No. 134, and this same number in the drawings cited above in Note 142.

(244) HIGHEST Grant of 11 May 1798, No 348; *Chronicle of the Russian Imperial Army*, compiled by Prince Dolgorukov, No. 133, and this same number in the drawings cited above in Note 142.

(245) HIGHEST Grant of 16 June 1799, No 518; *Chronicle of the Russian Imperial Army*, compiled by Prince Dolgorukov, No. 149, and this same number in the drawings cited above in Note 142.

(246) HIGHEST Grant of 11 May 1799, No 346; *Chronicle of the Russian Imperial Army*, compiled by Prince Dolgorukov, No. 136, and this same number in the drawings cited above in Note 142.

(247) HIGHEST Grant of 11 May 1799, No 342; *Chronicle of the Russian Imperial Army*, compiled by Prince Dolgorukov, No. 137, and this same number in the drawings cited above in Note 142.

(248) HIGHEST Grant of 11 May 1799, No 341; *Chronicle of the Russian Imperial Army*, compiled by Prince Dolgorukov, No. 132, and this same number in the drawings cited above in Note 142.

(249) HIGHEST Grant of 12 August 1799; *Chronicle of the Russian Imperial Army*, compiled by Prince Dolgorukov, No. 91, and this same number in the drawings cited above in Note 142.

(250) HIGHEST Grant of 25 October 1798; *Chronicle of the Russian Imperial Army*, compiled by Prince Dolgorukov, No. 104, and this same number in the drawings cited above in Note 142.

(251) HIGHEST Grant of 25 October 1798; *Chronicle of the Russian Imperial Army*, compiled by Prince Dolgorukov, No. 105, and this same number in the drawings cited above in Note 142.

(252) HIGHEST Grant of 25 October 1798; *Chronicle of the Russian Imperial Army*, compiled by Prince Dolgorukov, No. 106, and this same number in the drawings cited above in Note 142.

(253) HIGHEST Grant of 12 August 1799, No 971; *Chronicle of the Russian Imperial Army*, compiled by Prince Dolgorukov, No. 113, and this same number in the drawings cited above in Note 142.

(254) HIGHEST Grant of 12 August 1799, No 970; *Chronicle of the Russian Imperial Army*, compiled by Prince Dolgorukov, No. 112, and this same number in the drawings cited above in Note 142.

(255) HIGHEST Grant of 12 August 1799, No 978; *Chronicle of the Russian Imperial Army*, compiled by Prince Dolgorukov, No. 124, and this same number in the drawings cited above in Note 142.

(256) HIGHEST Grant of 22 April 1799, No 311; *Chronicle of the Russian Imperial Army*, compiled by Prince Dolgorukov, No. 100, and this same number in the drawings cited above in Note 142.

(257) HIGHEST Grant of 19 July 1798; *Chronicle of the Russian Imperial Army*, compiled by Prince Dolgorukov, No. 99, and this same number in the drawings cited above in Note 142.

(258) HIGHEST Grant of 13 June 1798; *Chronicle of the Russian Imperial Army*, compiled by Prince Dolgorukov, No. 97, and this same number in the drawings cited above in Note 142.

(259) HIGHEST Grant of 11 May 1799, No 343; *Chronicle of the Russian Imperial Army*, compiled by Prince Dolgorukov, No. 101, and this same number in the drawings cited above in Note 142

(260) *Chronicle of the Russian Imperial Army*, compiled by Prince Dolgorukov, No. 98, and this same number in the drawings cited above in Note 142

(261) HIGHEST Grant of 4 May 1798; *Chronicle of the Russian Imperial Army*, compiled by Prince Dolgorukov, No. 93, and this same number in the drawings cited above in Note 142.

(262) HIGHEST Grant of 7 December 1797; *Chronicle of the Russian Imperial Army*, compiled by Prince Dolgorukov, No. 96, and this same number in the drawings cited above in Note 142.

(263) HIGHEST Grant of 12 August 1799, No 979; *Chronicle of the Russian Imperial Army*, compiled by Prince Dolgorukov, No. 125, and this same number in the drawings cited above in Note 142.

(264) HIGHEST Grant of 12 August 1799, No 983; *Chronicle of the Russian Imperial Army*, compiled by Prince Dolgorukov, No. 130, and this same number in the drawings cited above in Note 142.

(265) HIGHEST Grant of 12 August 1799, No 980; *Chronicle of the Russian Imperial Army*, compiled by Prince Dolgorukov, No. 126, and this same number in the drawings cited above in Note 142.

(266) HIGHEST Grant of 12 August 1799, No 932; *Chronicle of the Russian Imperial Army*, compiled by Prince Dolgorukov, No. 129, and this same number in the drawings cited above in Note 142.

(267) HIGHEST Grant of 12 August 1799, No 981; *Chronicle of the Russian Imperial Army*, compiled by Prince Dolgorukov, No. 127, and this same number in the drawings cited above in Note 142.

(268) HIGHEST Grant of 12 August 1799, No 989; *Chronicle of the Russian Imperial Army*, compiled by Prince Dolgorukov, No. 146, and this same number in the drawings cited above in Note 142.

(269) HIGHEST Grant of 12 August 1799, No 984; *Chronicle of the Russian Imperial Army*, compiled by Prince Dolgorukov, No. 141, and this same number in the drawings cited above in Note 142.

(270) HIGHEST Grant of 12 August 1799, No 985; *Chronicle of the Russian Imperial Army*, compiled by Prince Dolgorukov, No. 142, and this same number in the drawings cited above in Note 142.

(271) HIGHEST Grant of 12 August 1799, No 986; *Chronicle of the Russian Imperial Army*, compiled by Prince Dolgorukov, No. 143, and this same number in the drawings cited above in Note 142.

(272) HIGHEST Grant of 12 August 1799, No 987; *Chronicle of the Russian Imperial Army*, compiled by Prince Dolgorukov, No. 144, and this same number in the drawings cited above in Note 142

(273) HIGHEST Grant of 12 August 1799, No 988; *Chronicle of the Russian Imperial Army*, compiled by Prince Dolgorukov, No. 145, and this same number in the drawings cited above in Note 142.

(274) HIGHEST Grant of 12 August 1799, No 974; *Chronicle of the Russian Imperial Army*, compiled by Prince Dolgorukov, No. 116, and this same number in the drawings cited above in Note 142.

(275) HIGHEST Grant of 12 August 1799, No 972; *Chronicle of the Russian Imperial Army*, compiled by Prince Dolgorukov, No. 114, and this same number in the drawings cited above in Note 142.

(276) HIGHEST Grant of 12 August 1799, No 975; *Chronicle of the Russian Imperial Army*, compiled by Prince Dolgorukov, No. 118, and this same number in the drawings cited above in Note 142.

(277) HIGHEST Grant of 25 October 1798; *Chronicle of the Russian Imperial Army*, compiled by Prince Dolgorukov, No. 117, and this same number in the drawings cited above in Note 142.

(278) HIGHEST Grant of 12 August 1799, No 976; *Chronicle of the Russian Imperial Army*, compiled by Prince Dolgorukov,

No. 119, and this same number in the drawings cited above in Note 142.

(279) HIGHEST Grant of 12 August 1799, No 977; *Chronicle of the Russian Imperial Army*, compiled by Prince Dolgorukov, No. 120, and this same number in the drawings cited above in Note 142.

(280) HIGHEST Grant of 16 June 1799, No 523; *Chronicle of the Russian Imperial Army*, compiled by Prince Dolgorukov, No. 150, and this same number in the drawings cited above in Note 142.

(281) HIGHEST Grant of 16 June 1799, No 519; *Chronicle of the Russian Imperial Army*, compiled by Prince Dolgorukov, No. 151, and this same number in the drawings cited above in Note 142.

(282) HIGHEST Grant of 16 June 1799, No 521; *Chronicle of the Russian Imperial Army*, compiled by Prince Dolgorukov, No. 152, and this same number in the drawings cited above in Note 142.

(283) HIGHEST Grant of 16 June 1799, No 520; *Chronicle of the Russian Imperial Army*, compiled by Prince Dolgorukov, No. 153, and this same number in the drawings cited above in Note 142.

(284) HIGHEST Grant of 11 May 1799, No 345; *Chronicle of the Russian Imperial Army*, compiled by Prince Dolgorukov, No. 131, and this same number in the drawings cited above in Note 142.

(285) HIGHEST Grant of 30 July 1798; *Chronicle of the Russian Imperial Army*, compiled by Prince Dolgorukov, No. 139, and this same number in the drawings cited above in Note 142.

(286) HIGHEST Grant of 9 January 1798; *Chronicle of the Russian Imperial Army*, compiled by Prince Dolgorukov, No. 107, and this same number in the drawings cited above in Note 142.

(287) HIGHEST Grant of 10 January 1798; *Chronicle of the Russian Imperial Army*, compiled by Prince Dolgorukov, No. 128, and this same number in the drawings cited above in Note 142.

(288) HIGHEST Grant of 19 January 1798; *Chronicle of the Russian Imperial Army*, compiled by Prince Dolgorukov, No. 123, and this same number in the drawings cited above in Note 142.

(289) HIGHEST Grant of 16 June 1799, No 526; *Chronicle of the Russian Imperial Army*, compiled by Prince Dolgorukov, No. 155, and this same number in the drawings cited above in Note 142.

(290) Actual flags preserved in various arsenals, including the St.-Petersburg Arsenal, and drawings of these flags located in THE SOVEREIGN EMPEROR's Own Library in porfolio No 169.

(291) Ditto.

(292) Ditto.

(293) Ditto.

(294) Ditto.

(295) Ditto.

(296) The same sources as cited in Notes 290-295, and a HIGHEST Grant of 30 March 1800, No 225.

(297) HIGHEST Grant of 26 December 1800, No 691.

(298) HIGHEST Grant of 6 March 1800, No 162.

(299) HIGHEST Grant of 5 August 1800, No 457.

(300) HIGHEST Grant of 28 February 1800, No 139.

(301) HIGHEST Grant of 17 March 1800, No 189.

(302) HIGHEST Grant of 30 August 1800, No 495.

(303) HIGHEST Grant of 26 December 1800, No 692.

(304) HIGHEST Grant of 17 December 1800, No 683.

(305) HIGHEST Grant of 1 October 1800, No 551.

(306) HIGHEST Grant of 1 October 1800, No 551.

(307) HIGHEST Grant of 21 June 1800, No 362.

(308) HIGHEST Grant of 5 August 1800, No 458.

(309) HIGHESTGrant of 30 August 1800, No 494.

(310) HIGHEST Grant of 16 June 1800, No 353.

(311) HIGHEST Grant of 21 July 1800, No 479.

(312) HIGHEST Grant of 21 July 1800, No 480.

(313) HIGHEST Grant of 21 July 1800, No 481.

(314) HIGHEST Grant of 5 July 1800, No 396.

(315) HIGHEST Grant of 5 July 1800, No 397.

(316) For flags of the Senate Regiment see drawings from 1800 located in THE SOVEREIGN EMPEROR's Own Library in porfolio No 169, and for flags of Marklovskii's Regiment see the Highest Grant of 26 May 1800, No 351.

(317) HIGHEST Grant of 16 June 1800, No 352.

(318) Actual flags preserved in arsenals.

(319) Ditto.

(320) Ditto.

(321) Ditto.

(322) Ditto.

(323) Ditto.

(324) Actual standards preserved in various arsenals, including the St.-Petersburg Arsenal, and in the regiments themselves, and drawings of cuirassier standards located in THE SOVEREIGN EMPEROR's Own Library in porfolio No 332.

(325) HIGHEST Grant of 25 June 1798; *Chronicle of the Russian Imperial Army*, compiled by Prince Dolgorukov, No. 162, and this same number in the drawings cited above in Note 142.

(326) HIGHEST Grant of 20 June 1798; *Chronicle of the Russian Imperial Army*, compiled by Prince Dolgorukov, No. 163, and this same number in the drawings cited above in Note 142.

(327) HIGHEST Grant of 23 September 1798; *Chronicle of the Russian Imperial Army*, compiled by Prince Dolgorukov, No. 164, and this same number in the drawings cited above in Note 142.

(328) HIGHEST Grant of 9 January 1798; *Chronicle of the Russian Imperial Army*, compiled by Prince Dolgorukov, No. 165, and this same number in the drawings cited above in Note 142.

(329) HIGHEST Grant of 23 September 1798; *Chronicle of the Russian Imperial Army*, compiled by Prince Dolgorukov, No. 166, and this same number in the drawings cited above in Note 142.

(330) HIGHEST Grant of 26 February 1798; *Chronicle of the Russian Imperial Army*, compiled by Prince Dolgorukov, No. 167, and this same number in the drawings cited above in Note 142.

(331) HIGHEST Grant of 26 February 1798; *Chronicle of the Russian Imperial Army*, compiled by Prince Dolgorukov, No. 168, and this same number in the drawings cited above in Note 142.

(332) HIGHEST Grant of 26 February 1798; *Chronicle of the Russian Imperial Army*, compiled by Prince Dolgorukov, No. 169, and this same number in the drawings cited above in Note 142.

(333) HIGHEST Grant of 23 September 1798; *Chronicle of the Russian Imperial Army*, compiled by Prince Dolgorukov, No. 170, and this same number in the drawings cited above in Note 142.

(334) HIGHEST Grant of 26 February 1798; *Chronicle of the Russian Imperial Army*, compiled by Prince Dolgorukov, No. 171, and this same number in the drawings cited above in Note 142.

(335) HIGHEST Grant of 9 January 1798; *Chronicle of the Russian Imperial Army*, compiled by Prince Dolgorukov, No. 172, and this same number in the drawings cited above in Note 142.

(336) HIGHEST Grant of 23 September 1798; *Chronicle of the Russian Imperial Army*, compiled by Prince Dolgorukov, No. 173, and this same number in the drawings cited above in Note 142.

(337) HIGHEST Grant of 10 February 1798; *Chronicle of the Russian Imperial Army*, compiled by Prince Dolgorukov, No. 174, and this same number in the drawings cited above in Note 142.

(338) HIGHEST Grant of 23 September 1798; *Chronicle of the Russian Imperial Army*, compiled by Prince Dolgorukov, No. 175, and this same number in the drawings cited above in Note 142.

(339) HIGHEST Grant of 11 February 1798; *Chronicle of the Russian Imperial Army*, compiled by Prince Dolgorukov, No. 176, and this same number in the drawings cited above in Note 142.

(340) HIGHEST Grant of 11 February 1798; *Chronicle of the Russian Imperial Army*, compiled by Prince Dolgorukov, No. 177, and this same number in the drawings cited above in Note 142.

(341) HIGHEST Grant of 199 July 1799, No 925; *Chronicle of the Russian Imperial Army*, compiled by Prince Dolgorukov, No. 196, and this same number in the drawings cited above in Note 142.

(342) HIGHEST Grant of 19 July 1799, No 923; *Chronicle of the Russian Imperial Army*, compiled by Prince Dolgorukov, No. 197, and this same number in the drawings cited above in Note 142.

(343) HIGHEST Grant of 19 July 1799, No 924; *Chronicle of the Russian Imperial Army*, compiled by Prince Dolgorukov, No. 198, and this same number in the drawings cited above in Note 142.

(344) Actual standards preserved in various arsenals, including the St.-Petersburg Arsenal, and in the regiments themselves, and drawings of dragoon standards located in THE SOVEREIGN EMPEROR's Own Library in porfolio No 332.

(345) HIGHEST Grant of 21 January 1799, No 60; *Chronicle of the Russian Imperial Army*, compiled by Prince Dolgorukov, No. 178, and this same number in the drawings cited above in Note 142.

(346) HIGHEST Grant of 7 December 1797; *Chronicle of the Russian Imperial Army*, compiled by Prince Dolgorukov, No. 179, and this same number in the drawings cited above in Note 142.

(347) HIGHEST Grant of 21 January 1798, No 59; *Chronicle of the Russian Imperial Army*, compiled by Prince Dolgorukov, No. 180, and this same number in the drawings cited above in Note 142.

(348) HIGHEST Grant of 6 September 1798; *Chronicle of the Russian Imperial Army*, compiled by Prince Dolgorukov, No.

181, and this same number in the drawings cited above in Note 142.

(349) HIGHEST Grant of 26 March 1798; *Chronicle of the Russian Imperial Army*, compiled by Prince Dolgorukov, No. 182, and this same number in the drawings cited above in Note 142.

(350) HIGHEST Grant of 25 April 1798; *Chronicle of the Russian Imperial Army*, compiled by Prince Dolgorukov, No. 183, and this same number in the drawings cited above in Note 142.

(351) HIGHEST Grant of 21 January 1799, No 58; *Chronicle of the Russian Imperial Army*, compiled by Prince Dolgorukov, No. 184, and this same number in the drawings cited above in Note 142.

(352) HIGHEST Grant of 20 November 1797; *Chronicle of the Russian Imperial Army*, compiled by Prince Dolgorukov, No. 185, and this same number in the drawings cited above in Note 142.

(353) HIGHEST Grant of 20 November 1797; *Chronicle of the Russian Imperial Army*, compiled by Prince Dolgorukov, No. 186, and this same number in the drawings cited above in Note 142.

(354) HIGHEST Grant of 20 November 1797; *Chronicle of the Russian Imperial Army*, compiled by Prince Dolgorukov, No. 187, and this same number in the drawings cited above in Note 142.

(355) HIGHEST Grant of 4 May 1798; *Chronicle of the Russian Imperial Army*, compiled by Prince Dolgorukov, No. 188, and this same number in the drawings cited above in Note 142.

(356) HIGHEST Grant of 21 January 1799, No 61; *Chronicle of the Russian Imperial Army*, compiled by Prince Dolgorukov, No. 189, and this same number in the drawings cited above in Note 142.

(357) HIGHEST Grant of 3 May 1798; *Chronicle of the Russian Imperial Army*, compiled by Prince Dolgorukov, No. 190, and this same number in the drawings cited above in Note 142.

(358) HIGHEST Grant of 3 May 1798; *Chronicle of the Russian Imperial Army*, compiled by Prince Dolgorukov, No. 191, and this same number in the drawings cited above in Note 142.

(359) HIGHEST Grant of 26 February 1798; *Chronicle of the Russian Imperial Army*, compiled by Prince Dolgorukov, No. 192, and this same number in the drawings cited above in Note 142.

(360) HIGHEST Grant of 25 June 1798; *Chronicle of the Russian Imperial Army*, compiled by Prince Dolgorukov, No. 193, and this same number in the drawings cited above in Note 142.

(361) HIGHEST Grant of 19 July 1799, No 927; *Chronicle of the Russian Imperial Army*, compiled by Prince Dolgorukov, No. 199, and this same number in the drawings cited above in Note 142.

(362) HIGHEST Grant of 19 July 1799, No 926; *Chronicle of the Russian Imperial Army*, compiled by Prince Dolgorukov, No. 200, and this same number in the drawings cited above in Note 142.

(363) Actual standards preserved in arsenals, and some in the regiments themselves.

(364) HIGHEST Grant of 26 May 1800, No 350.

(365) HIGHEST Grant of 16 June 1800, No 356.

(366) HIGHEST Grant of 22 June 1800, No 367.

(367) Actual standards preserved in the St.-Petersburg Arsenal, and drawings located in THE SOVEREIGN EMPEROR's Own Library in books No 158 and No 159.

(368) *Chronicle of the Russian Imperial Army*, compiled by Prince Dolgorukov, No. 1; this same number in the drawings cited above in Note 142, and the flags themselves preserved in the St.-Petersburg Arsenal.

(369) *Chronicle of the Russian Imperial Army*, compiled by Prince Dolgorukov, No. 3; this same number in the drawings cited above in Note 142, and the flags themselves preserved in the St.-Petersburg Arsenal.

(370) *Chronicle of the Russian Imperial Army*, compiled by Prince Dolgorukov, No. 5; this same number in the drawings cited above in Note 142, and the flags themselves preserved in the St.-Petersburg Arsenal.

(371) Statements by contemporaries and actual flags preserved in the St.-Petersburg Arsenal.

(372) *Chronicle of the Russian Imperial Army*, compiled by Prince Dolgorukov, No. 2; and this same number in the drawings cited above in Note 142, and the flags themselves preserved in the St.-Petersburg Arsenal.

(373) *Chronicle of the Russian Imperial Army*, compiled by Prince Dolgorukov, No. 4; this same number in the drawings cited above in Note 142, and the flags themselves preserved in the St.-Petersburg Arsenal.

(374) *Chronicle of the Russian Imperial Army*, compiled by Prince Dolgorukov, No. 6; this same number in the drawings cited above in Note 142, and the flags themselves preserved in the St.-Petersburg Arsenal.

(375) Table of flags from 1800, locatedin THE SOVEREIGN EMPEROR's Own Library in portfolio No 169, and flags prepared but never used, preserved in the St.-Petersburg Arsenal.

(376) *Chronicle of the Russian Imperial Army*, compiled by Prince Dolgorukov, No. 160; this same number in the drawings cited above in Note 142, and a standard itself preserved in HIS IMPERIAL MAJESTY's Own Arsenal in the Anichkov Palace.

(377) Actual standards preserved in the St.-Petersburg Arsenal.

(378) The poles of these standards, with St.-George crosses and ribbons from 1813 hanging on them, are preserved in HER MAJES-

TY's Cavalier Guards Regiment. The cloth field, however, has been destroyed by time and their drawings are nowhere to be found.

(379) Drawings located in THE SOVEREIGN EMPEROR's Own Library, catalogued under No 159.

(380) Actual standards preserved in the St.-Petersburg Arsenal.

(381) *Chronicle of the Russian Imperial Army*, compiled by Prince Dolgorukov, No. 161, and this same number in the drawings cited above in Note 142.

(382) *Chronicle of the Russian Imperial Army*, compiled by Prince Dolgorukov, No. 203; this same number in the drawings cited above in Note 142, and actual flags preserved in HIS IMPERIAL HIGHNESS GRAND DUKE MICHAEL PAVLOVICH's Own Arsenal.

(383) HIGHESTGrant of 6 June 1799, No 500. However, it is highly probable that this grant was given for the preceding flags.

(384) Information received from the 1st Cadet Corps; *Chronicle of the Russian Imperial Army*, compiled by Prince Dolgorukov, No. 7, and this same number in the drawings cited above in Note 142.

(385) *Chronicle of the Russian Imperial Army*, compiled by Prince Dolgorukov, No. 201; this same number in the drawings cited above in Note 142; a drawing sent from the Ural Host, and a HIGHESTGrant of 19 April 1798.

(386) *Chronicle of the Russian Imperial Army*, compiled by Prince Dolgorukov, Nos. 204 and 205; these same numbers in the drawings cited above in Note 142, and a HIGHESTGrant of 10 August 1798.

(385) In the *Chronicle of the Russian Imperial Army*, compiled by Prince Dolgorukov, No. 202, it is written in regard to the Leib-Ural Sotnia's flags: *"Raspberry flag. On it a white cross. From the number of Preobrazhenskii flags personally presented by HIS IMPERIAL MAJESTY on 4 January 1799."* In these words is a clear contradiction, since the *raspberry* flags of the Life-Guards Preobrazhenskii Regiment were presented later, on 6 January 1799, and had in their corners gold wreathes with the inscription *"Blagodat'."* In a table of flags and standards compiled by Prince Dolgorukov himself for the Chronicle citee above and located in THE SOVEREIGN EMPEROR's Own Library, catalogued under No 332, the Leib-Ural flag is depicted without monograms or inscriptions. With this in mind, from what Prince Dolgorukov presents it can only be concluded that the Leib-Ural Sotnia's flag was taken from that number being prepared for the Life-Guards Preobrazhenskii Regiment and which did not yet have the afore-mentioned monograms and insriptions.

(386) Drawing of flags sent from the Don Host, and a HIGHESTGrant of 15 February 1800, No 93.

(389) *Chronicle of the Russian Imperial Army*, compiled by Prince Dolgorukov, Nos. 206 and 207; these same numbers in the drawings cited above in Note 142, and actual flags of the Lithuanian-Tatar Regiment preserved in the St.-Petersburg Arsenal, and a HIGHEST Grant of 15 September 1798.

(390) *Chronicle of the Russian Imperial Army*, compiled by Prince Dolgorukov, No 156, and this same number in the drawings cited above in Note 142.

(391) *Chronicle of the Russian Imperial Army*, compiled by Prince Dolgorukov, No 157, and this same number in the drawings cited above in Note 142.

(392) *Chronicle of the Russian Imperial Army*, compiled by Prince Dolgorukov, No 158, and this same number in the drawings cited above in Note 142.

(393) *Chronicle of the Russian Imperial Army*, compiled by Prince Dolgorukov, No 194, and this same number in the book with drawings of uniforms, flags, and standards located in THE SOVEREIGN EMPEROR's Own Library, catalogued under No 177.

(394) *Chronicle of the Russian Imperial Army*, compiled by Prince Dolgorukov, No 195, and this same number in the book with drawings of uniforms, flags, and standards located in THE SOVEREIGN EMPEROR's Own Library, catalogued under No 177.

(395) HIGHEST Grant of 16 February 1800, No 96. In this grant it was stated that the flag was being awarded for distinction shown by the Duke de Bourbon's Regiment *at Constance*, while a report from Genealissimus Prince Suvorov in Lindau to EMPEROR PAUL I dated 9/20 October 1799 said, "The Prince de Condé notifies me that on 27 September/8 October he was attacked by the French at *Costnits*, where he battled for seven hours against an enemy twice his number, but in the end was forced to retire after losing about 200 men killed, about 50 missing, and 4 officers. His wounded numbered about 500. The cnemy lost over 300 men killed and 30 privates and 2 officers taken prisoner, and a flag was captured."

(396) *Chronicle of the Russian Imperial Army*, compiled by Prince Dolgorukov, No 159; this same number in the drawings cited above in Note 142, and actual flags preserved in the St.-Petersburg Arsenal.

(397) PSZ, Vol. XXIV, pg. 5, No 17,547.

(398) PSZ, Vol. XXV, pg. 551, No 18,848.

(399) PSZ, Vol. XXVI, pg. 338, No 19,594.

(400) HIGHEST Order of 16 June 1799 and a list of distinctions held by the forces, compiled in the Inspection Department of the War Ministry.

(401) The list cited in the above note.

(402) Journal of the Riga (sic, should be Ryazhsk, i.e. *Rizhskii* misprinted for *Ryazhskii* – M.C.) Infantry Regiment, signed by its *Chef*, Lieut.-Gen. Graf Langeron, presented to the State Military Collegium in a report dated 24 August 1824, No 514.

РИСУНКИ

Одежды и Вооруженія

РОССІЙСКИХЪ

ВОЙСКЪ.

PLATES LIST OF ILLUSTRATIONS

1248. Flag granted to the Taurica Grenadier Regiment, 30 March 1800.

1249. Standards granted to His Majesty's Leib-Cuirassier Regiment, 25 June 1798.

1250. Standards granted to Cuirassier regiments: a-b. Her Majesty's, 1798; c-d. Military Order, 1798; e-f. Yekaterinoslav, 1798; g-h. Kazan, 1798; i-k. Ryazan, 1798; l-m. Yamburg, 1798.

1251. Standards granted to Cuirassier regiments: a-b. Glukhov, 1798; c-d. Kiev, 1798; e-f. Nezhin, 1798; g-h. Sofiya, 1798; i-k. Starodub, 1798; l-m. Chernigov, 1798.

1252. Standards granted to Cuirassier regiments: a-b. Riga, 1798; c-d. Kharkov, 1798; e-f. Little Russia, 1798; g-h. Friderici's, 1799; i-k. Neplyuev's, 1798; l-m. Zorn's, 1799.

1253. Standards granted to the Vladimir Dragoon Regiment, 21 January 1799.

1254. Standards granted to Dragoon regiments: a-b. Astrakhan, 1797; c-d. Nizhnii-Novgorod, 1799; e-f. Pskov, 1798; g-h. St. Petersburg, 1798; i-k. Smolensk, 1798; l-m. Taganrog, 1799.

1255. Standards granted to Dragoon regiments: a-b. Irkutsk, 1797; c-d. Orenburg, 1797; e-f. Sibieria, 1797; g-h. Ingermanland, 1798; i-k. Narva, 1799; l-m. Rostov, 1798.

1256. Standards granted to Dragoon regiments: a-b. Moscow, 1798; c-d. Seversk, 1798; e-f. Kargopol, 1798; g-h. Schreider's, 1799; i-k. Khastatov's, 1799.

1257. Standards granted in 1800 to the Dragoon Regiments of Skalon, Pushkin, and Obrezkov.

1258. Flags granted to Life-Guards regiments in December 1796. a. Preobrazhenskii, b. Semenovskii, c. Izmailovskii. Note: These flags were granted without Maltese crosses, which were sewn on later, in 1798.

1259. Flags granted to *Chef* batg. in the Life Guards, 2 January 1798. a. Preobrazhenskii, b. Semenovskii, c. Izmailovskii.

1260. Flags granted to *Chef* battalions in the Life Guards, 2 January 1798. a. Preobrazhenskii, b. Semenovskii, c. Izmailovskii.

1261. Flags granted to Life-Guards regiments, 7 January 1799. a. Preobrazhenskii, b. Semenovskii, c. Izmailovskii.

1262. Flags granted to Life-Guards regiments, 7 January 1799. a. Preobrazhenskii, b. Semenovskii, c. Izmailovskii.

1263. Flags intended for the Life-Guards Preobrazhenskii, Semenovskii, and Izmailovskii Regiments, 1800.

1264. Cavalier-Guards Standards. a. Cavalier Guards Corps, granted in 1799; b. Cavalier Guards Regiment, granted in 1800; c. Cavalier Guards Regiment, granted in 1800.

1265. Standards granted to Life-Guards reg.: a-b. Horse, 1796; c-d. Horse, 1798; e-f. Horse, 1799; g-h. Cossack, 1799.

1266. Flags granted to the Army (later 1st) Cadet Corps, 2 November 1798.

1267. Flag granted to the Ural Host, 19 April 1798.

1268. Flags granted to Cossack troops: a. 1st Chuguev Regiment, 10 August 1798; b. 2nd Chuguev Regiment, 10 August 1798; c. Leib-Ural Sotnia, 4 January 1799.

1269. Flag granted to the Don Host, 15 February 1800.

1270. Flags granted to Horse regiments, 15 September 1798: a-b. Lithuanian, Tatar; c-d. Polish.

1271. Flags and standards granted to regiments in the Prince de Condé's Corps, 15 January 1798: a-b. Prince de Condé's French Noble Regiment; c-d. Duke de Bourbon's Grenadier Regiment; e-f. Duke de Hohenlohe's German Regiment; g-h. Duke de Berry's Noble Dragoon Regiment; i-k. Duke d'Enghien's Dragoon Regiment.

1272. Flags granted to the Senate Battalion in 1799.

1273. Medals instituted for award to lower military ranks for twenty years' service without reproach. a. St. Anne, 12 November 1796; b. Donative of St. John of Jerusalem, 10 October 1800.

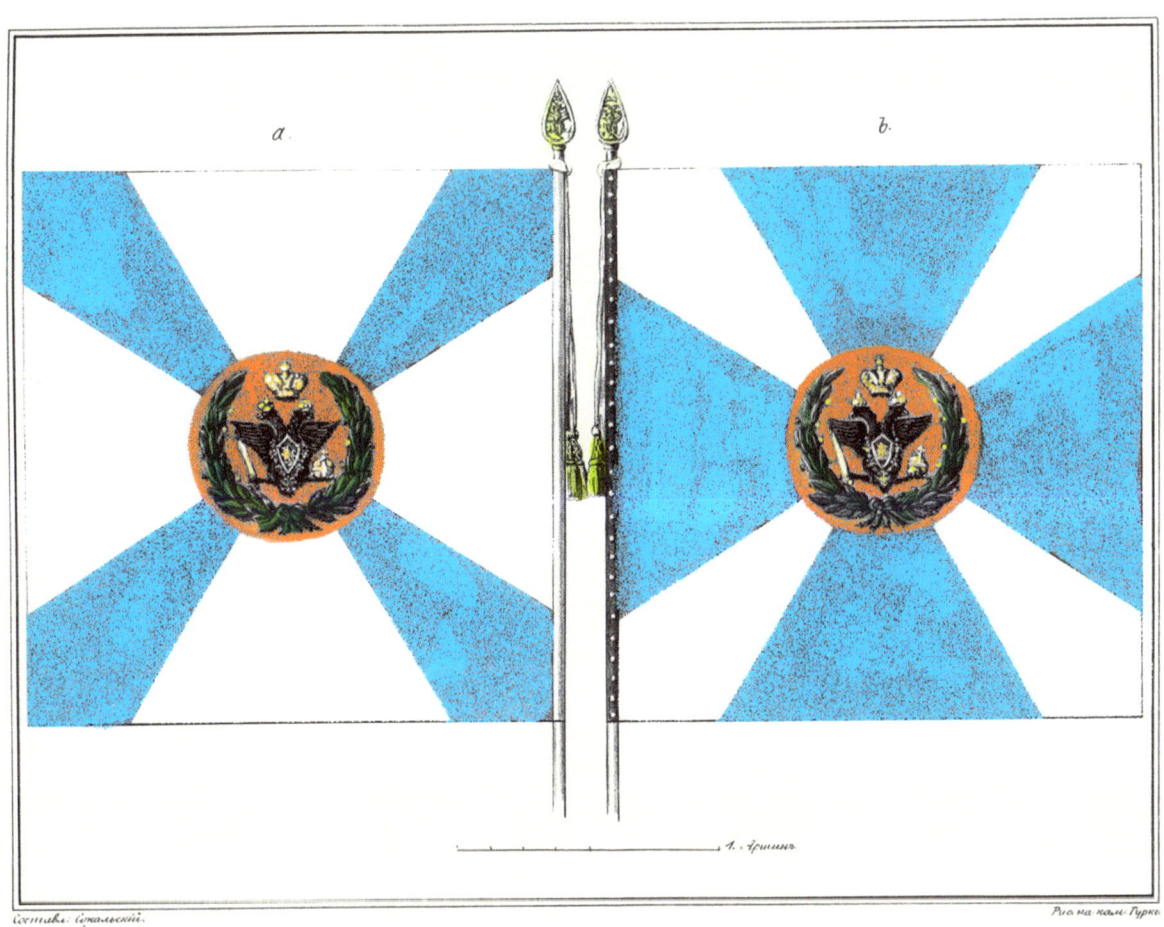

Flags granted to the Leib-Grenadier Regiment in 1797.

Spearhead and tassel with lace strap, established for flags in 1796.

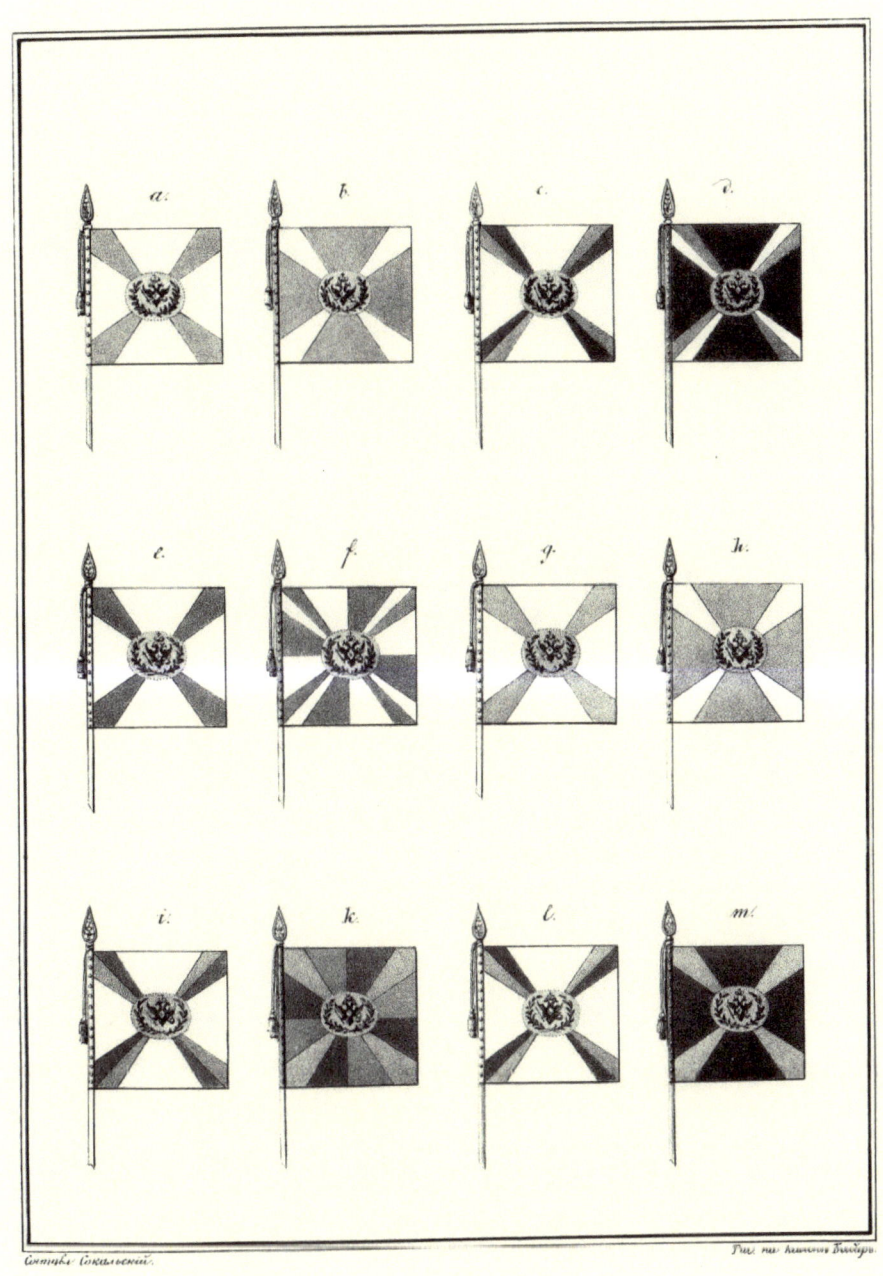

Flags granted to Grenadier regiments: a-b. Pavlovskii, 1797; c-d. Yekaterinoslav, 1798; e-f. St. Petersburg, 1798; g-h. Astrakhan, 1798; i-k. Kiev, 1798; l-m. Moscow, 1798.

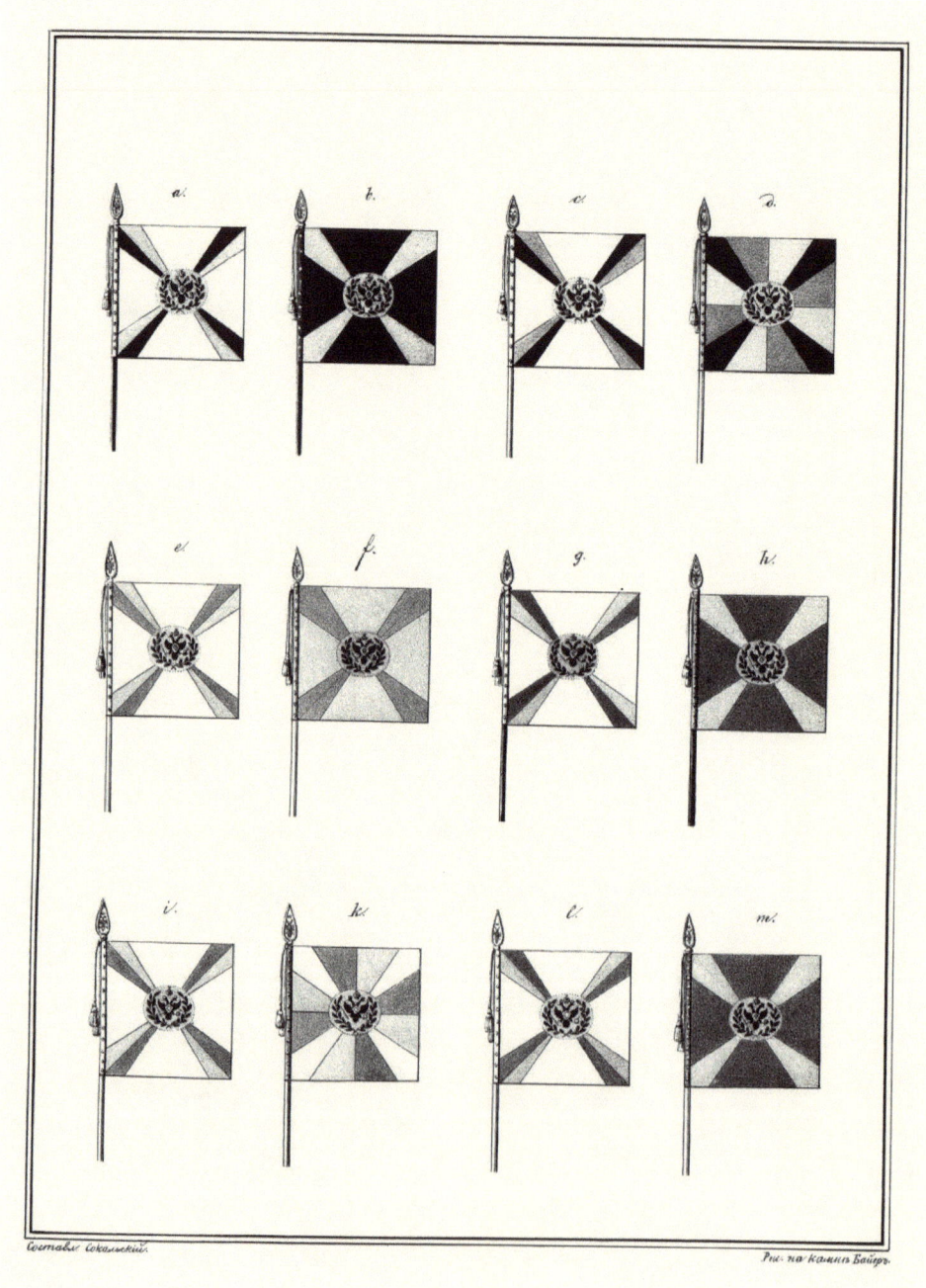

Flags granted to Grenadier regiments: a-b. Little Russia, 1798; c-d. Siberia, 1798; e-f. Phanagoria, 1798; g-h. Kherson, 1798; i-k. Taurica, 1798; l-m. Caucasus, 1798.

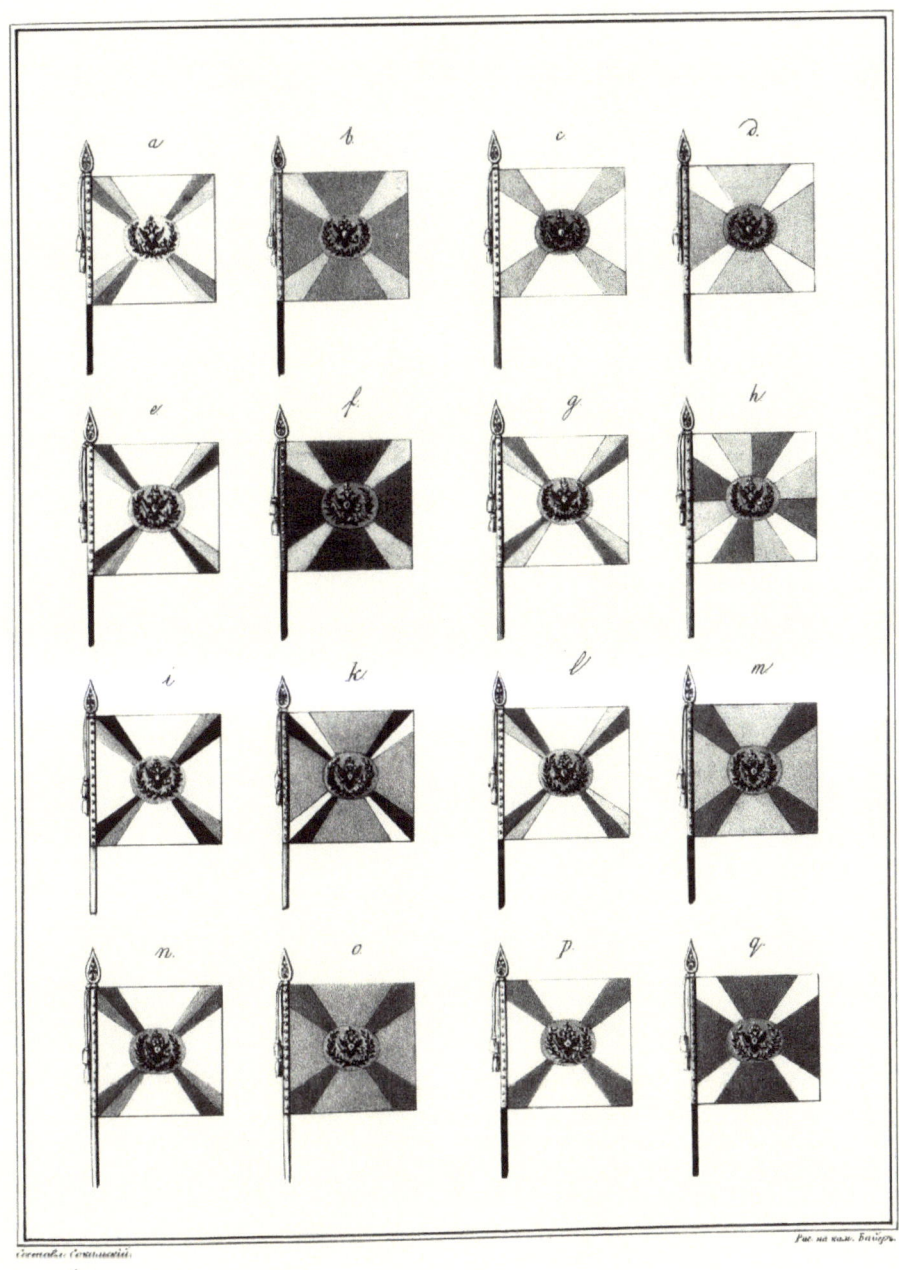

Flags granted to Musketeer reg. a-b. Belozersk, 1798; c-d. Nasheburg, 1797; e-f. Chernigov, 1798; g-h. New Ingermanland, 1798; i-k. Yaroslavl, 1797; l-m. Caucasus, 1798; n-o. Smolensk, 1798; p-q. Ryazhsk, 1797.

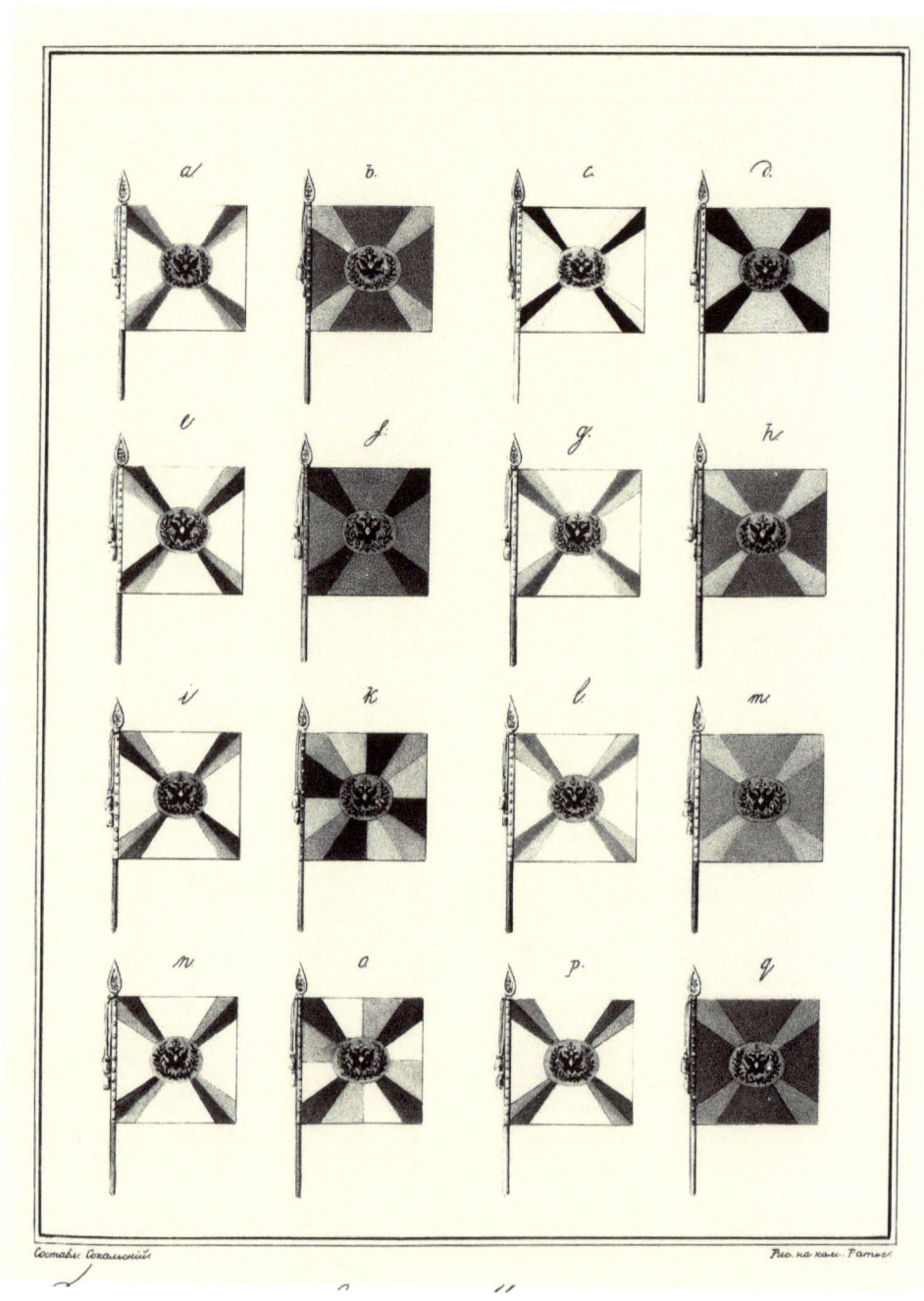

Flags granted to Musketeer regiments: a-b. Kursk, 1798; c-d. Kozlov, 1797; e-f. Sevastopol, 1799; g-h. Belev, 1799; i-k. Aleksopol, 1798; l-m. Schlüsselburg, 1798; n-o. Bryansk, 1798; p-q. Troitsk, 1799.

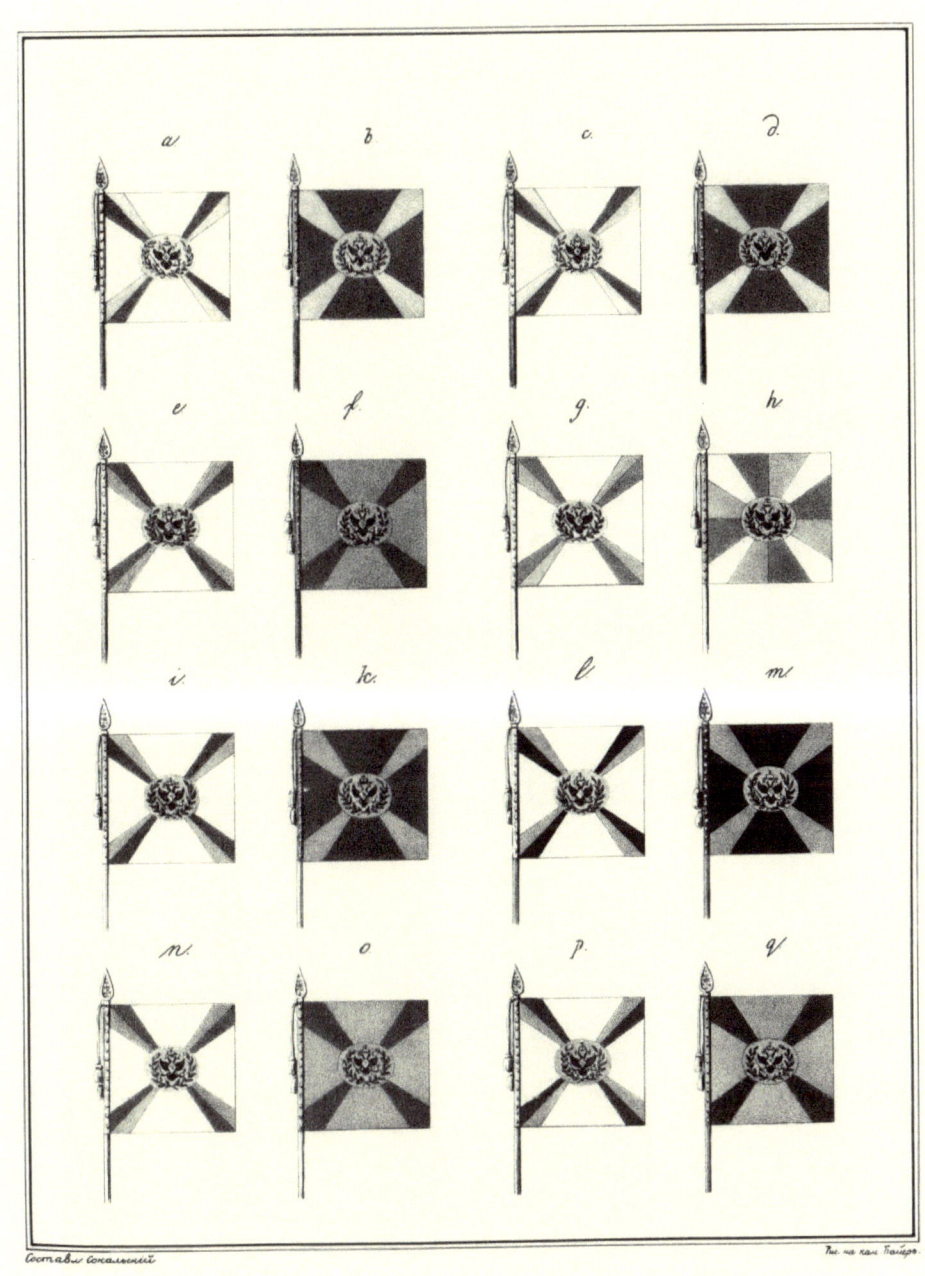

Flags granted to Musketeer regiments: a-b. Ladoga, 1798; c-d. Polotsk, 1798; e-f. Archangel, 1798; g-h. Old Ingermanland, 1797; i-k. Novgorod, 1798; l-m. Nizhnii-Novgorod, 1798; n-o. Vitebsk, 1799; p-q. Azov, 1798.

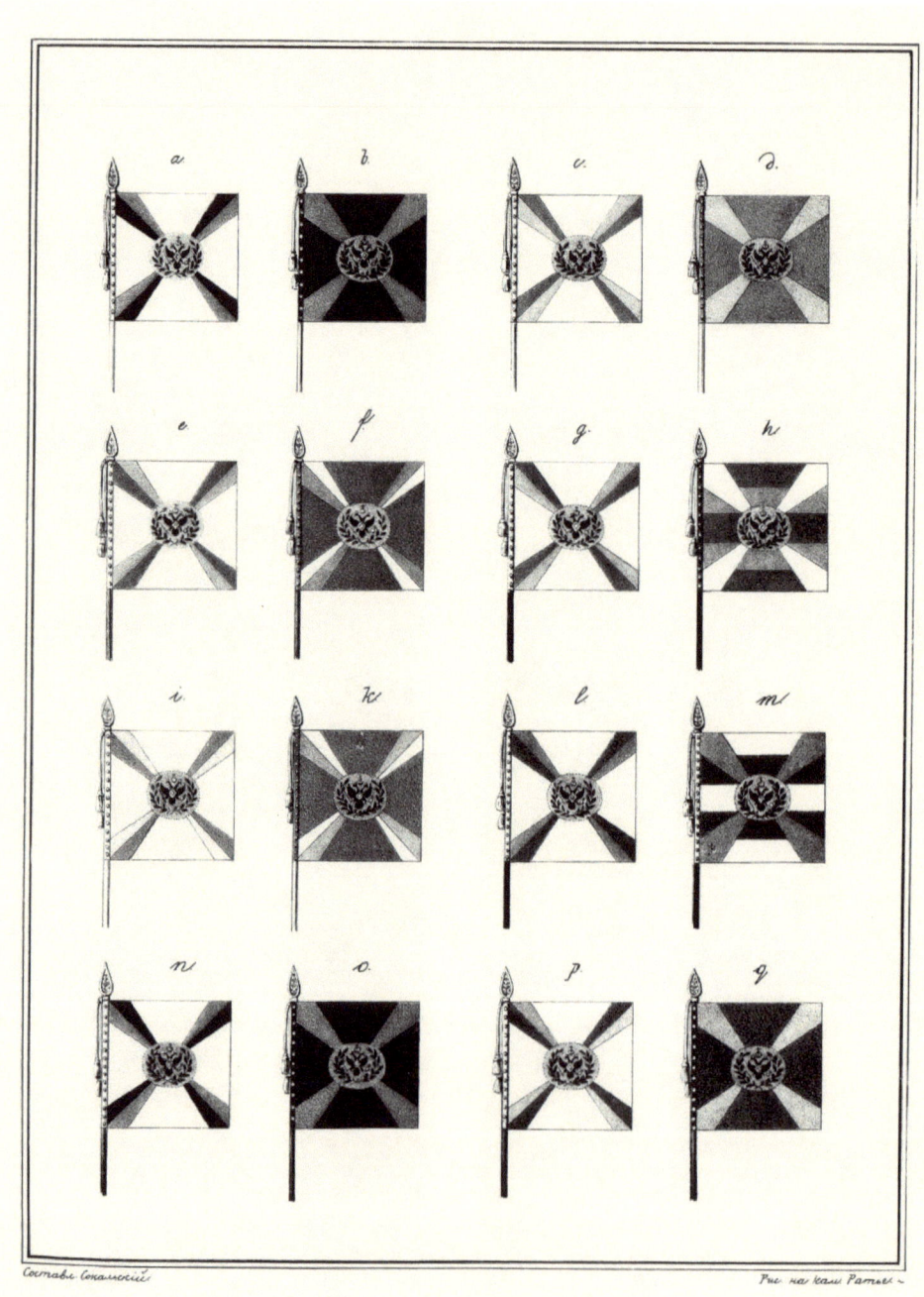

Flags granted to Musketeer regiments: a-b. Orel, 1798; c-d. Reval, 1798; e-f. Tula, 1797; g-h. Yelets, 1798; i-k. Pskov, 1797; l-m. Tambov, 1797; n-o. Rostov, 1798; p-q. Murom, 1797.

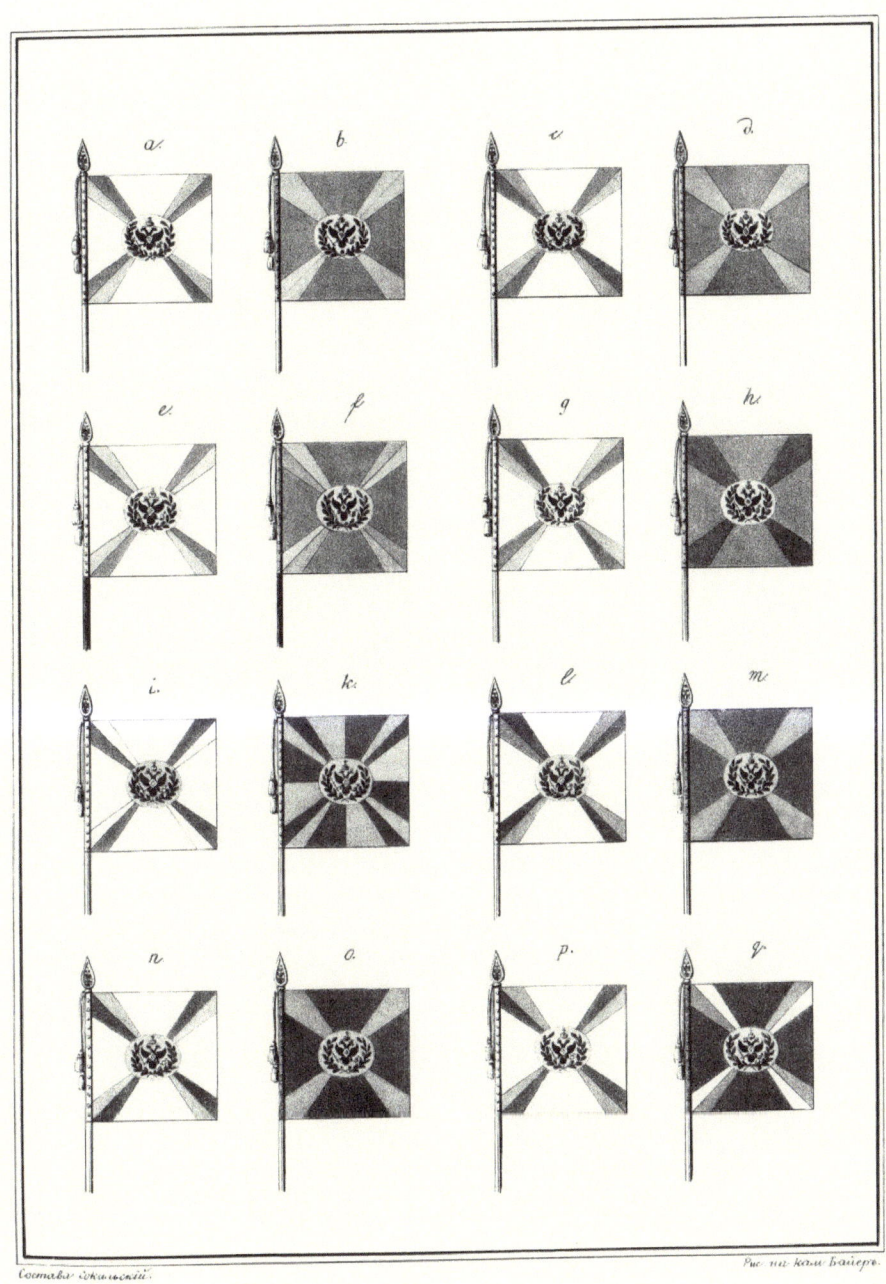

Flags granted to Musketeer regiments: a-b. Staryi Oskol, 1797; c-d. Tobolsk, 1798; e-f. Tiflis, 1799; g-h. Voronezh, 1798; i-k. Kazan, 1799; l-m. Moscow, 1798; n-o. Kabarda, 1799; p-q. Vladimir, 1798.

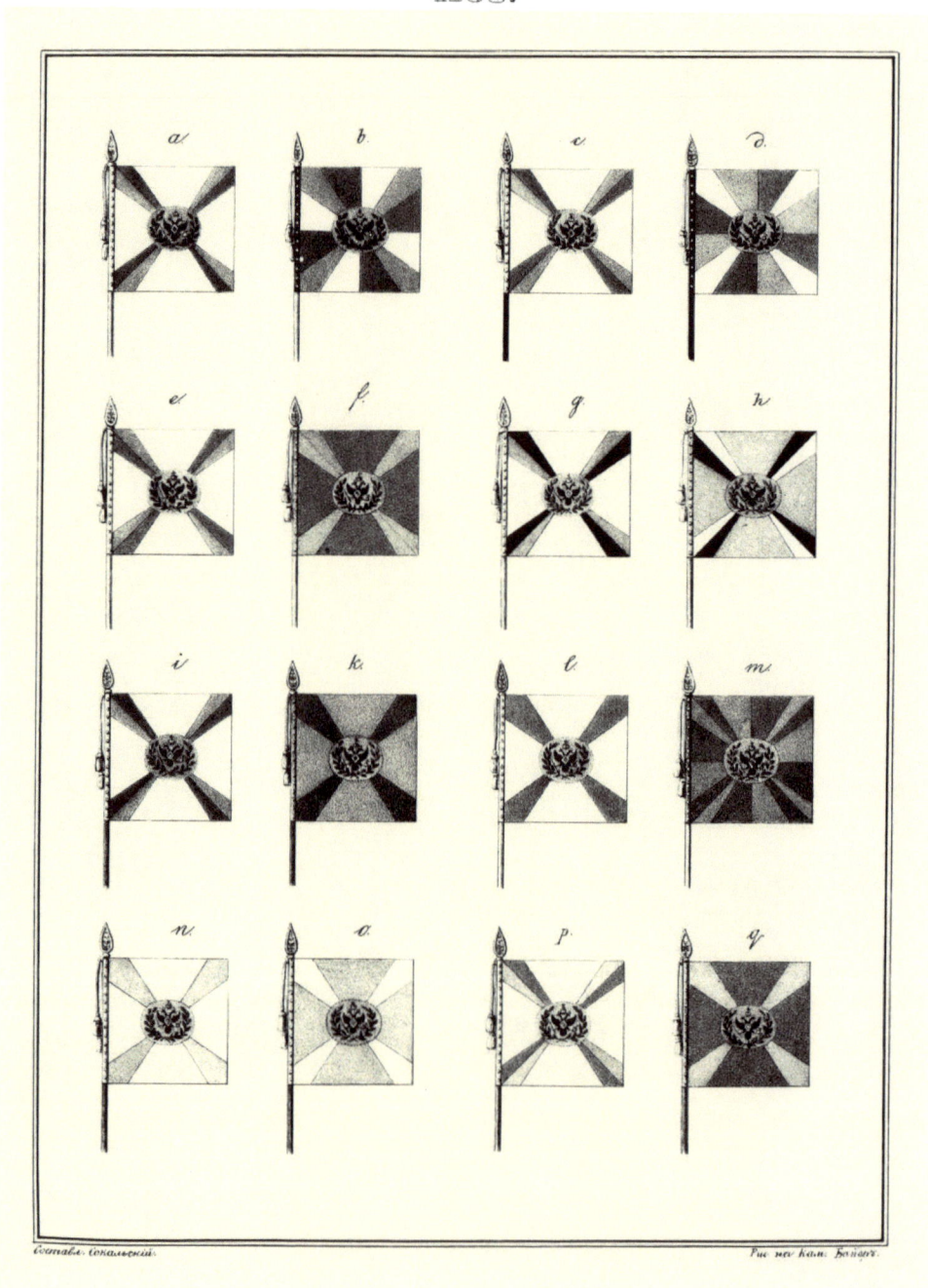

Flags granted to Musketeer regiments: a-b. Uglich, 1798; c-d. Sevsk, 1798; e-f. Narva, 1798; g-h. Dnieper, 1798; i-k. Vyatka, 1798; l-m. Suzdal, 1799; n-o. Kexholm, 1797; p-q. Viborg, 1798.

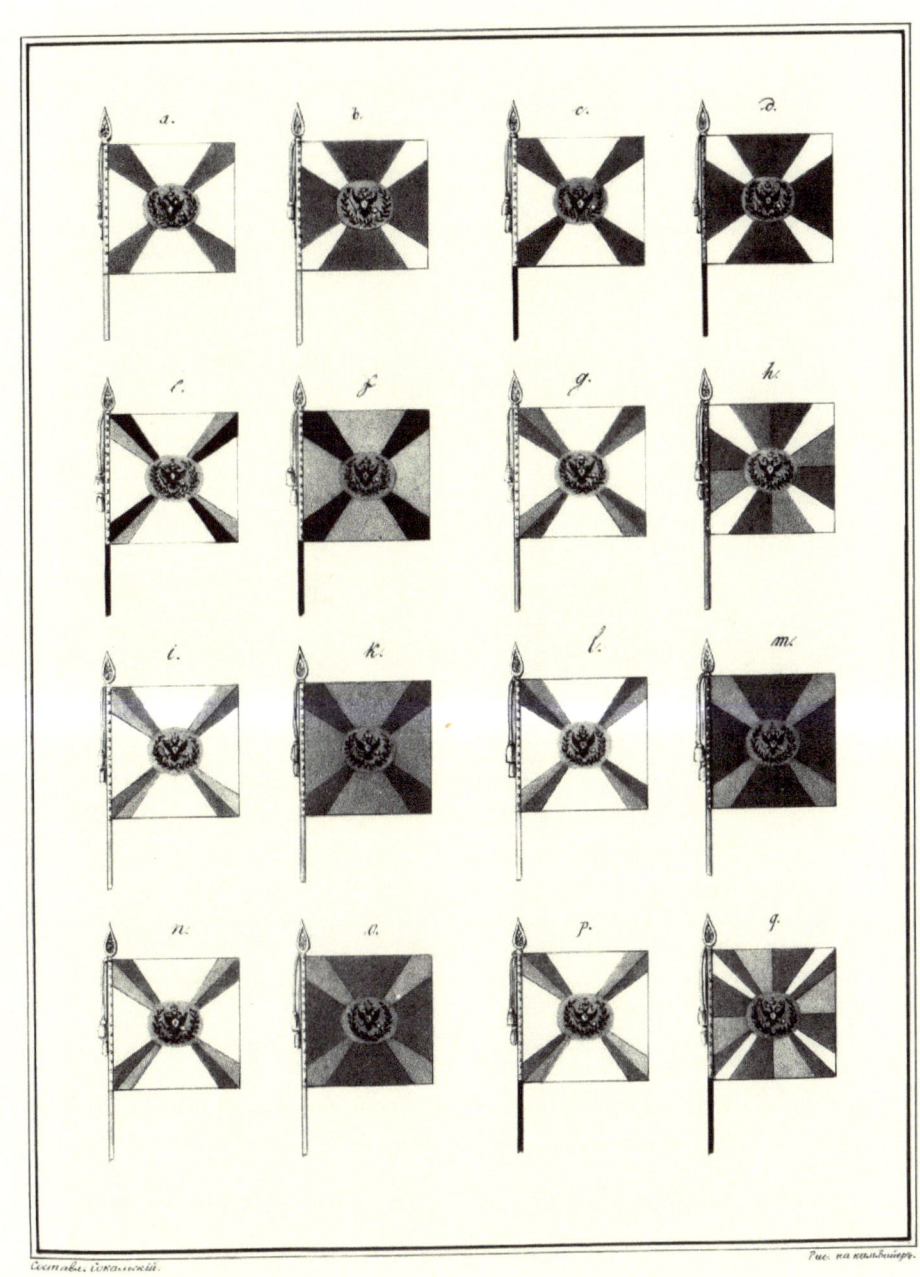

Flags granted to Musketeer regiments: a-b. Ryazan, 1798; c-d. Neva, 1798; e-f. Velikie Luki, 1797; g-h. Sofiya, 1798; i-k. Shirvan, 1799; l-m. Perm, 1798; n-o. Nizovsk, 1798; p-q. Butyrsk, 1798.

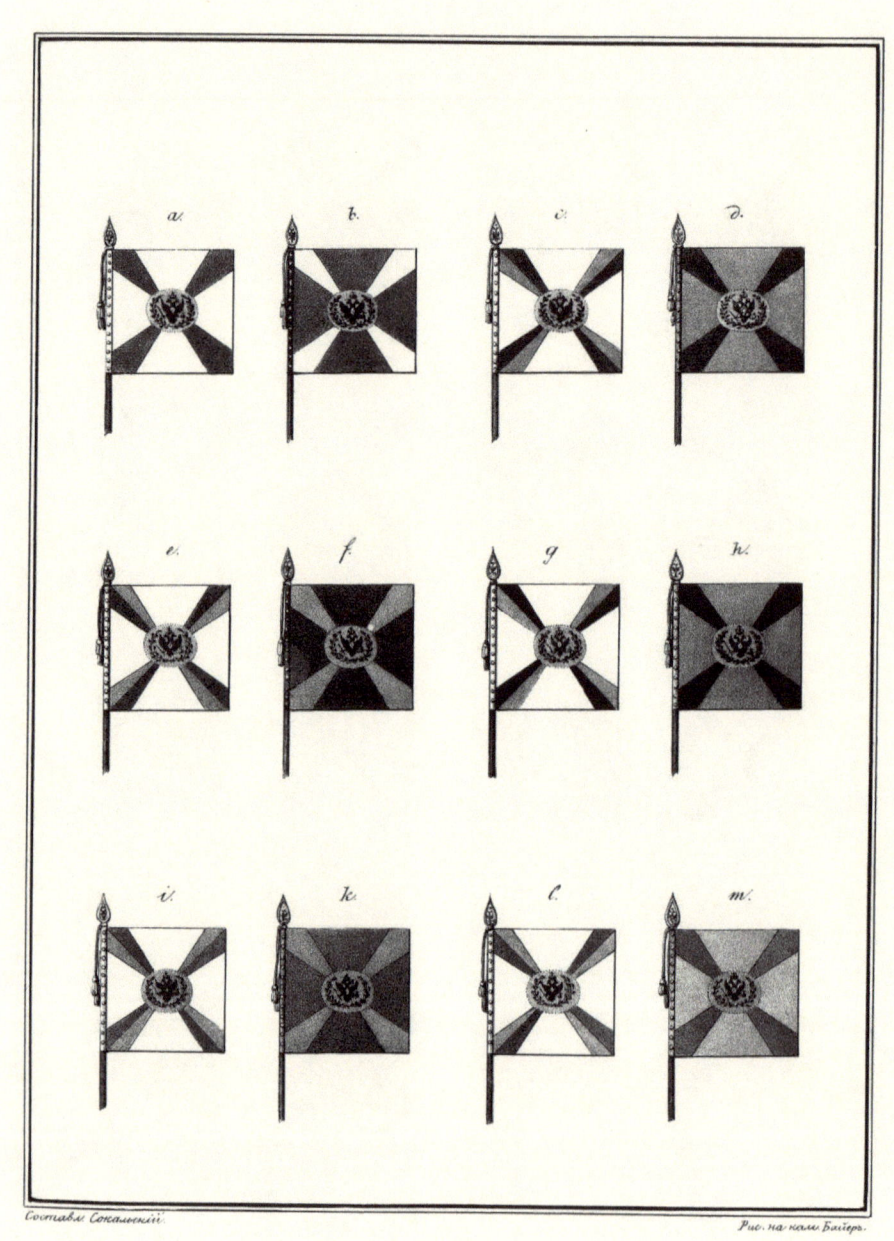

Flags granted to Musketeer regiments: a-b. Ufa, 1798; c-d. Rylsk, 1798; e-f. Yekaterinburg, 1798; g-h. Selenginsk, 1799; i-k. Tomsk, 1799; l-m. Arkharov's, 1797.

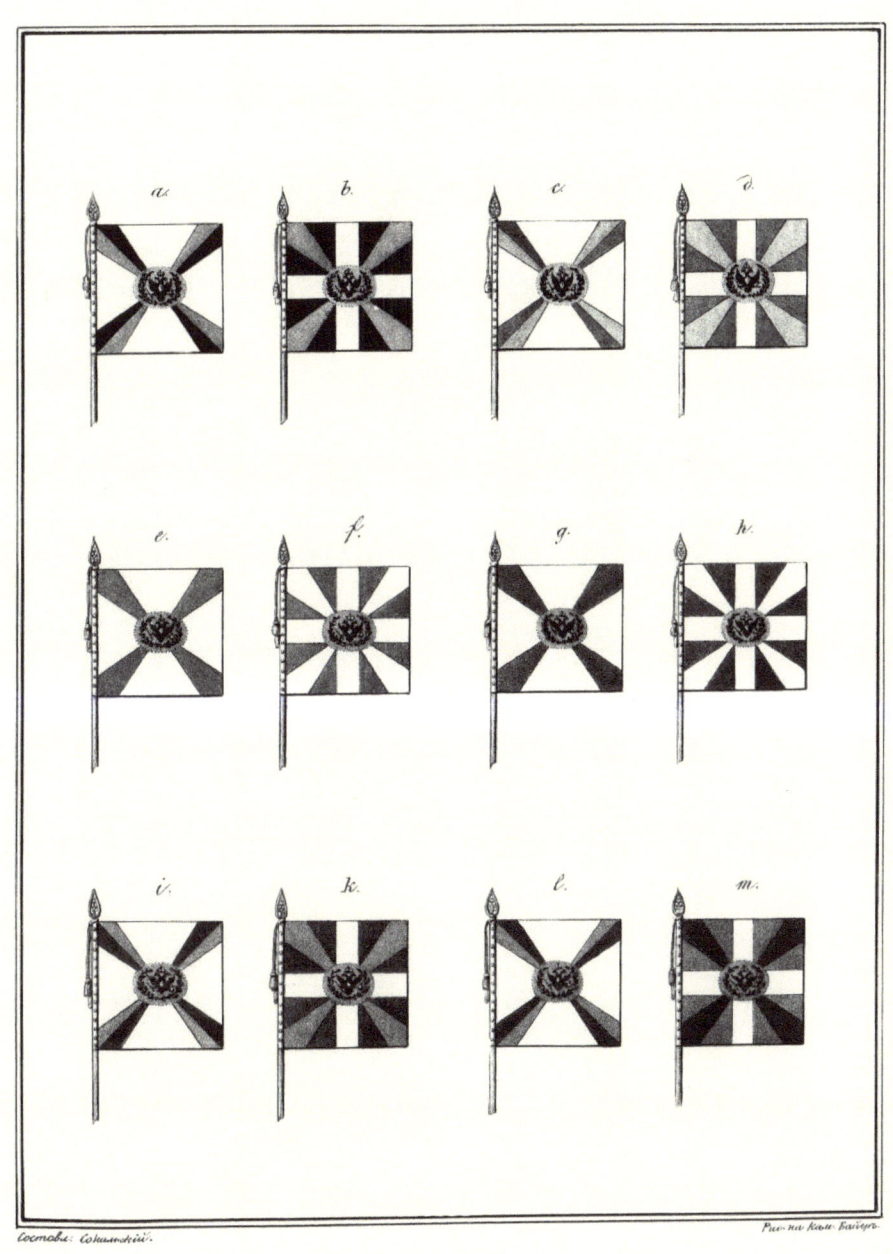

Flags granted to Musketeer regiments: a-b. Pavlutskii's, 1799; c-d. Leitern's, 1799; e-f. Brant's, 1799; g-h. Müller 1st's, 1799; i-k. Marklovskii's 1st's, 1799; l-m. Berg's, 1799.

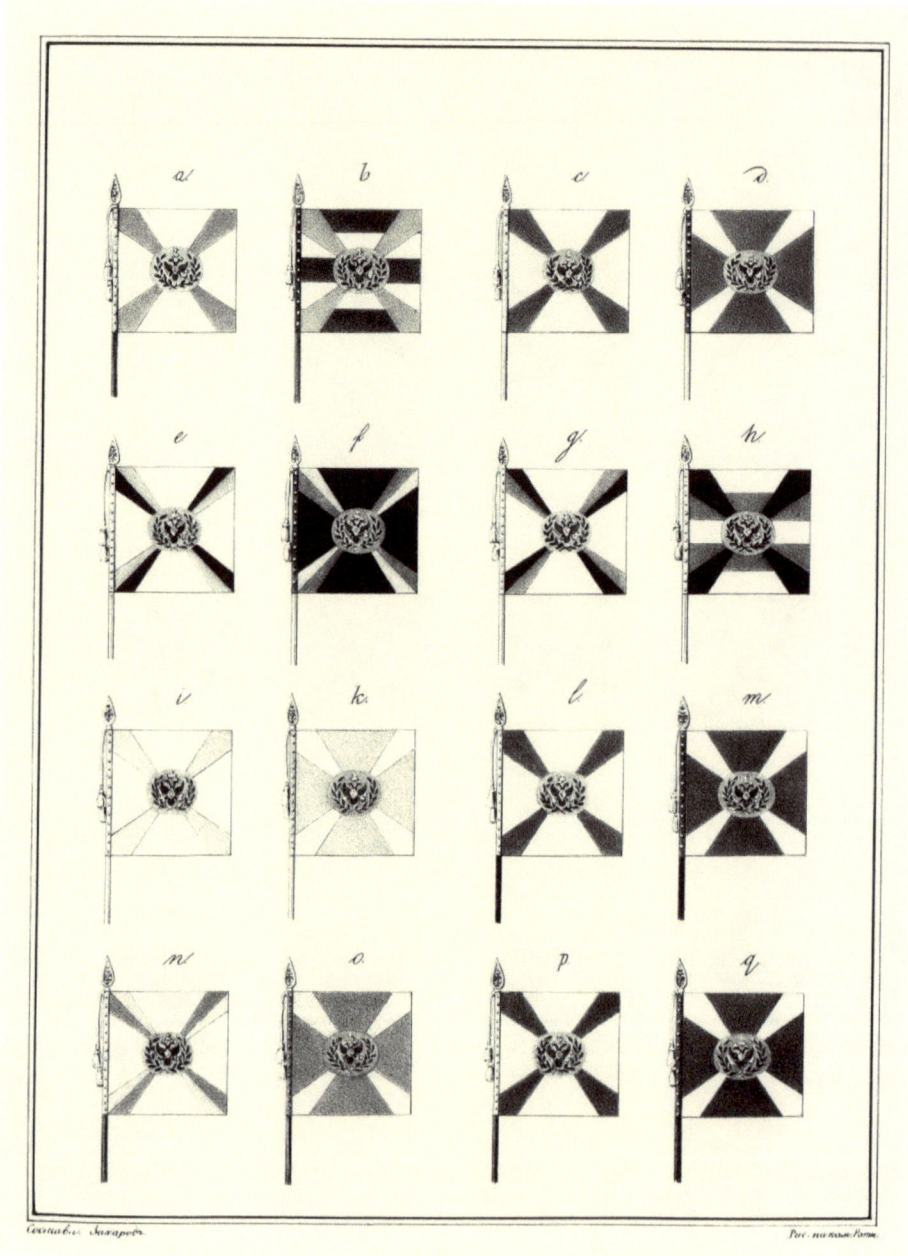

Flags granted to Garrison regiments: a-b. St. Petersburg, 1797; c-d. Moscow, 1798; e-f. Viborg, 1798; g-h. Fredrikshamn, 1798; i-k. Reval, 1798; l-m. Riga, 1798; n-o. Archangel, 1799; p-q. Kazan, 1798.

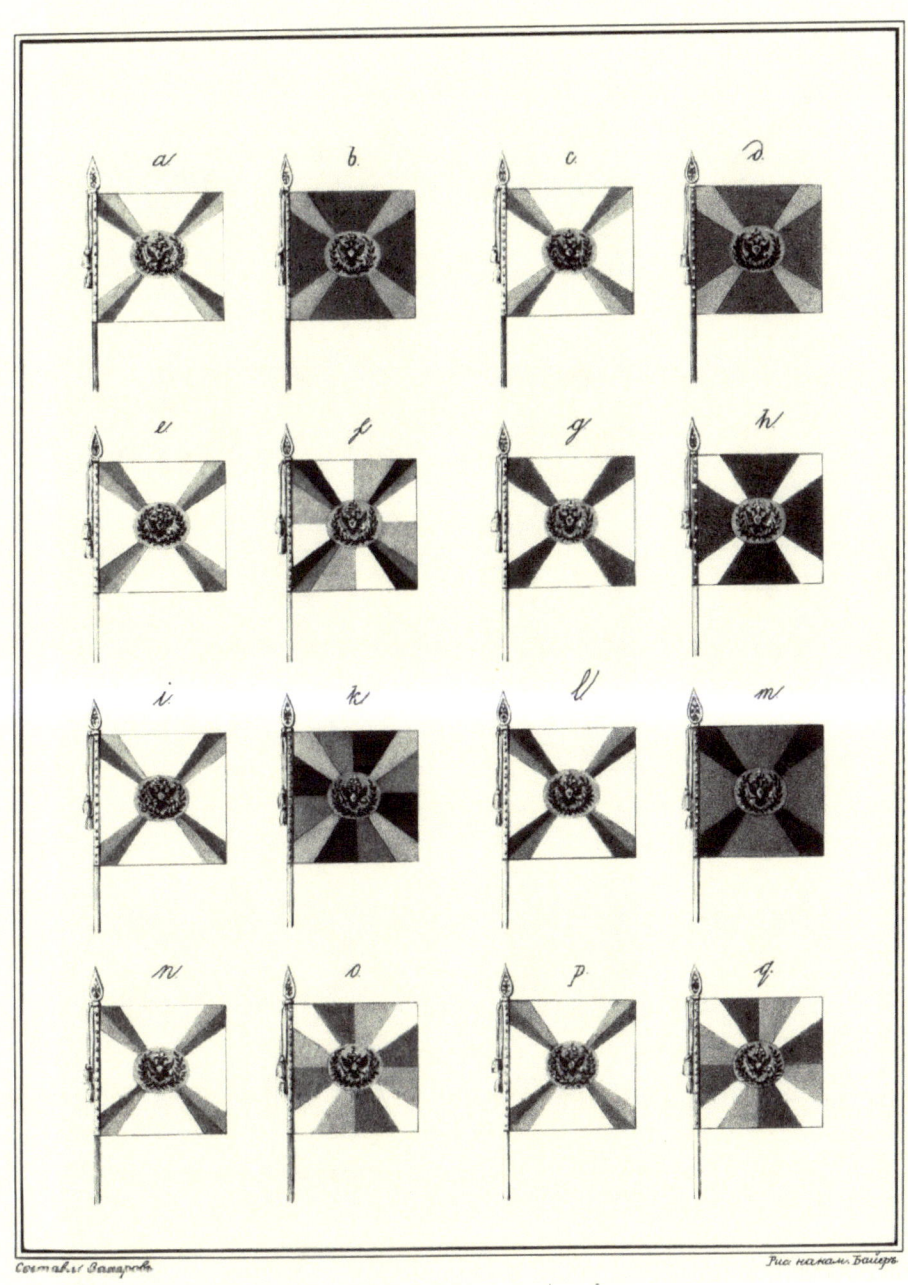

Flags granted to Garrison regiments: a-b. Orenburg, 1798; c-d. Tobolsk, 1799; e-f. Smolensk, 1799; g-h. Selenginsk, 1799; i-k. Kiev, 1798; l-m. Taganrog, 1799; n-o. Baltic, 1799; p-q. Dünamünde, 1799.

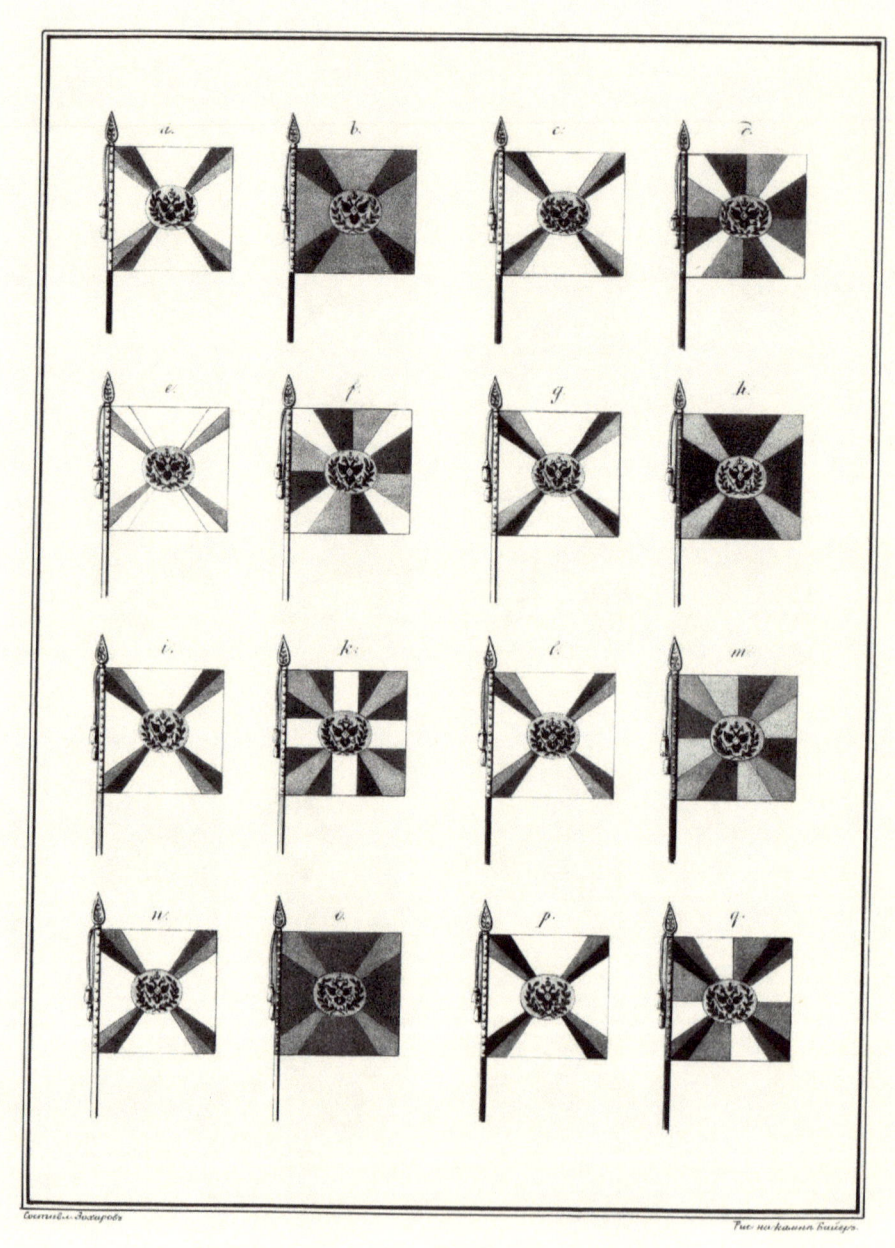

Flags granted to Garrison regiments: a-b. Irkutsk, 1799; c-d. Kronstadt, 1798; e-f. Narva, 1798; g-h. Yelisavetgrad, 1798; i-k. Dmitrii, 1799; l-m. Azov, 1798; n-o. Omsk, 1799; p-q. Astrakhan, 1799.

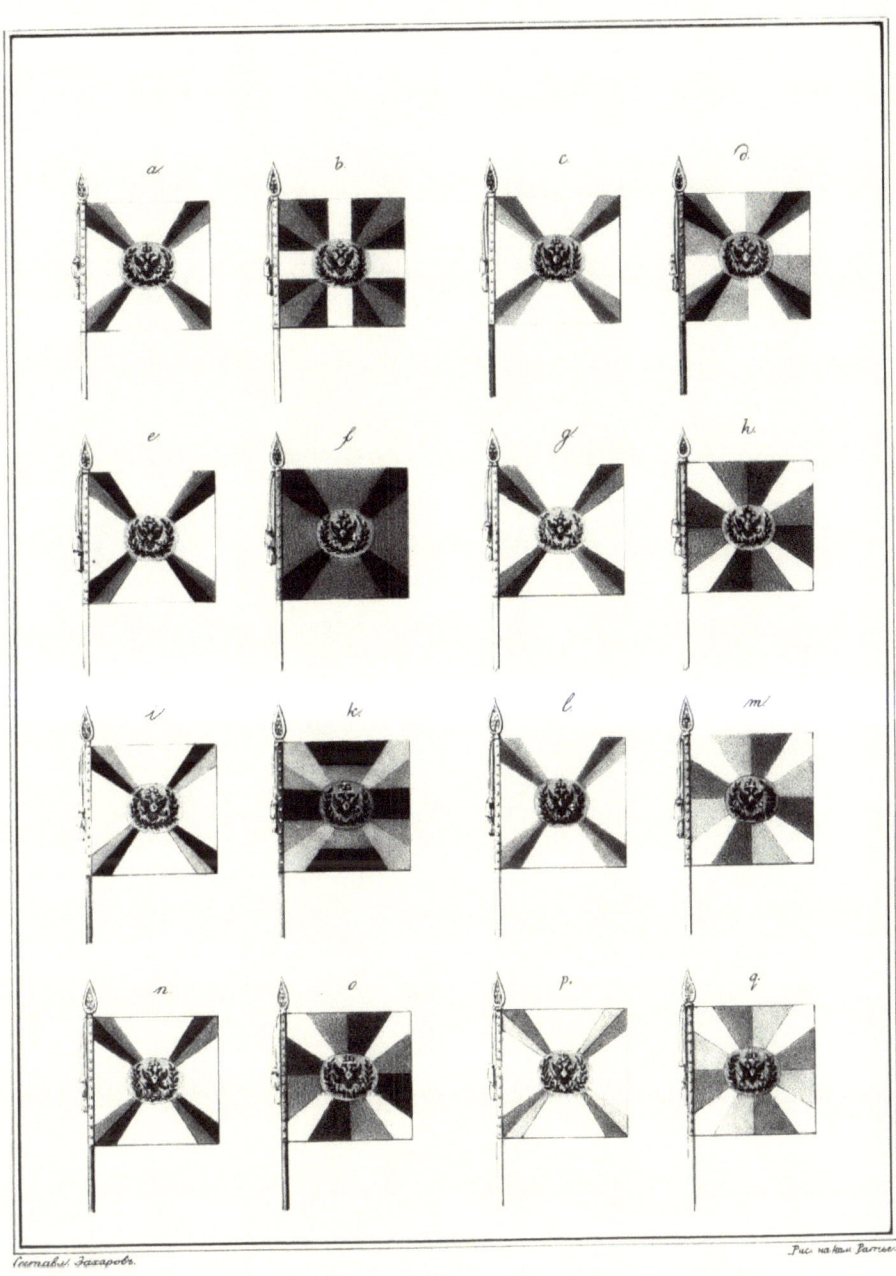

Flags granted to Garrison regiments: a-b. Tsaritsyn, 1799; c-d. Kizlyar, 1799; e-f. Schlüsselburg, 1799; g-h. Villmanstrand, 1798; i-k. Kexholm, 1798; l-m. Nyslot, 1798; n-o. Arensburg, 1799; p-q. Pernau, 1799.

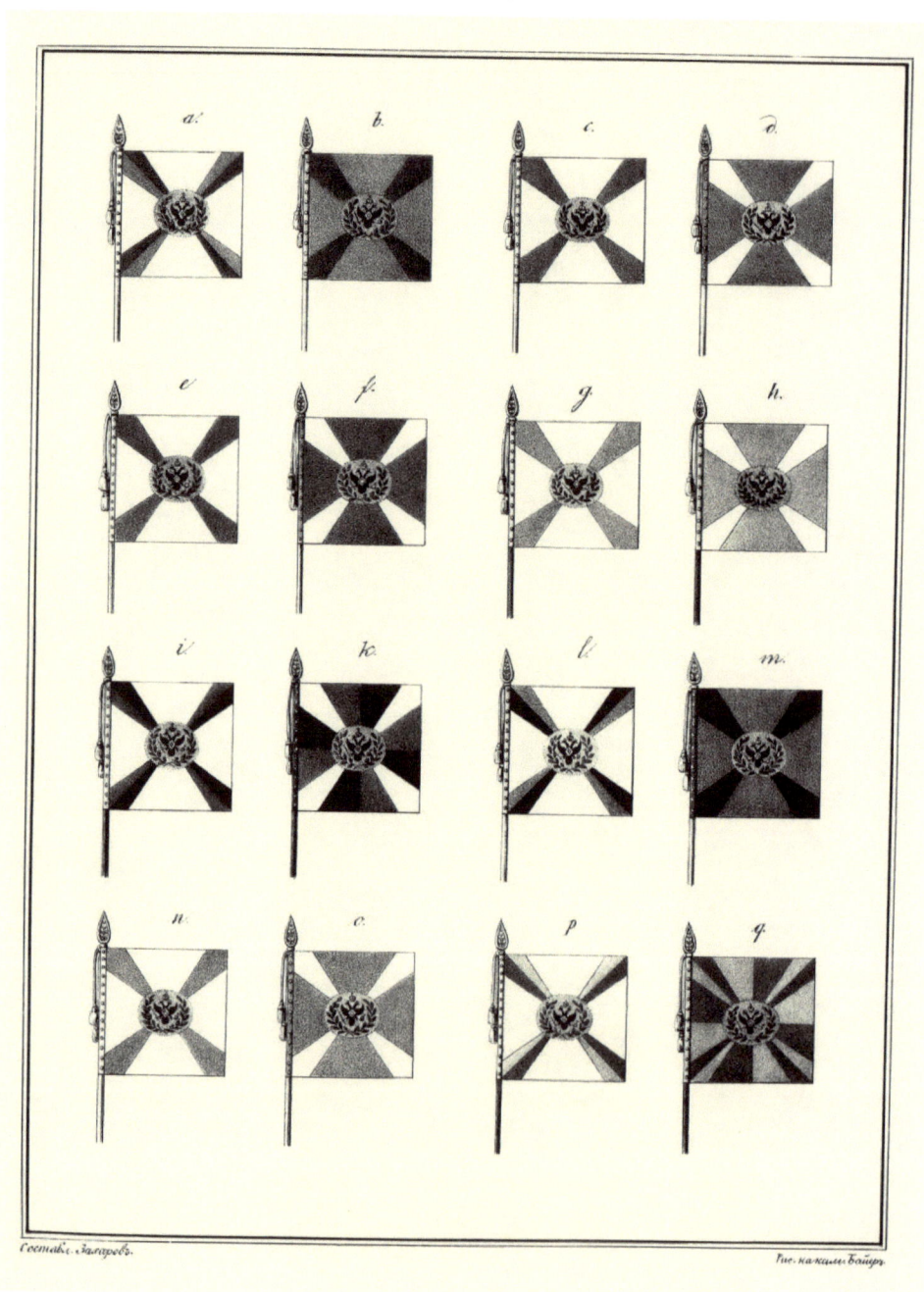

Flags granted to Garrison regiments: a-b. Bakhmut, 1799; c-d. Tambov, 1799; e-f. Voronezh, 1798; g-h. Vladimr, 1798; i-k. Simbirsk, 1799; l-m. Nizhnii-Novgorod, 1797; n-o. Novgorod, 1798; p-q. Tver, 1797.

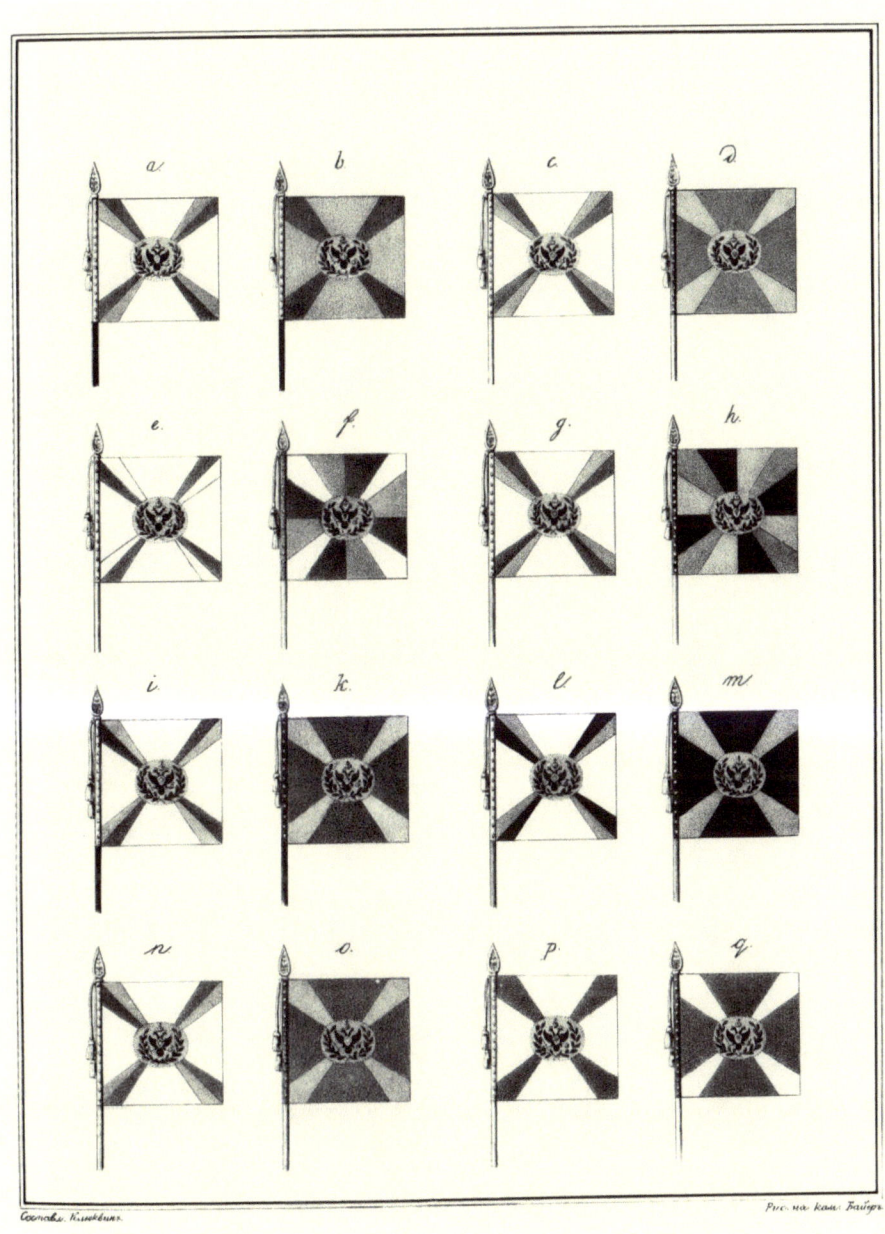

Flags granted to Garrison regiments: a-b. Aleksandrovsk, 1799; c-d. Sudak, 1799; e-f. Petrovsk, 1799; g-h. Balaklava, 1799; i-k. Perekop, 1799; l-m. Stavropol, 1799; n-o. Orsk (n.d.). p-q. Kizilsk, 1799.

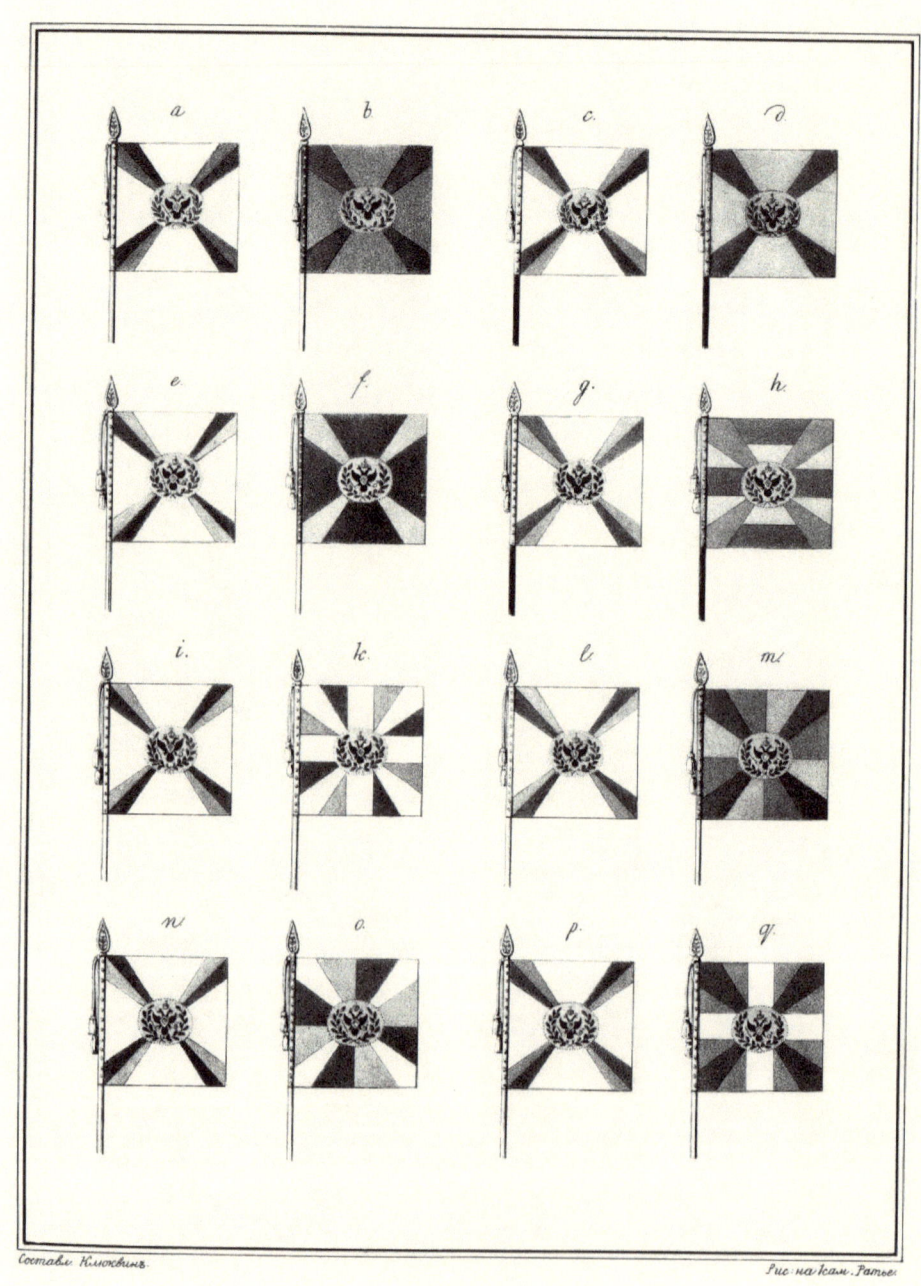

Flags granted to Garrison regiments: a-b. Verkhneuralsk, 1799; c-d. Troitsk, 1799; e-f. Zver-inogolovsk, 1799; g-h. Pskov, 1799; i-k. Dünaburg, 1799; l-m. Vitebsk, 1799; n-o. Polotsk, 1798; p-q. Rogachev, 1799.

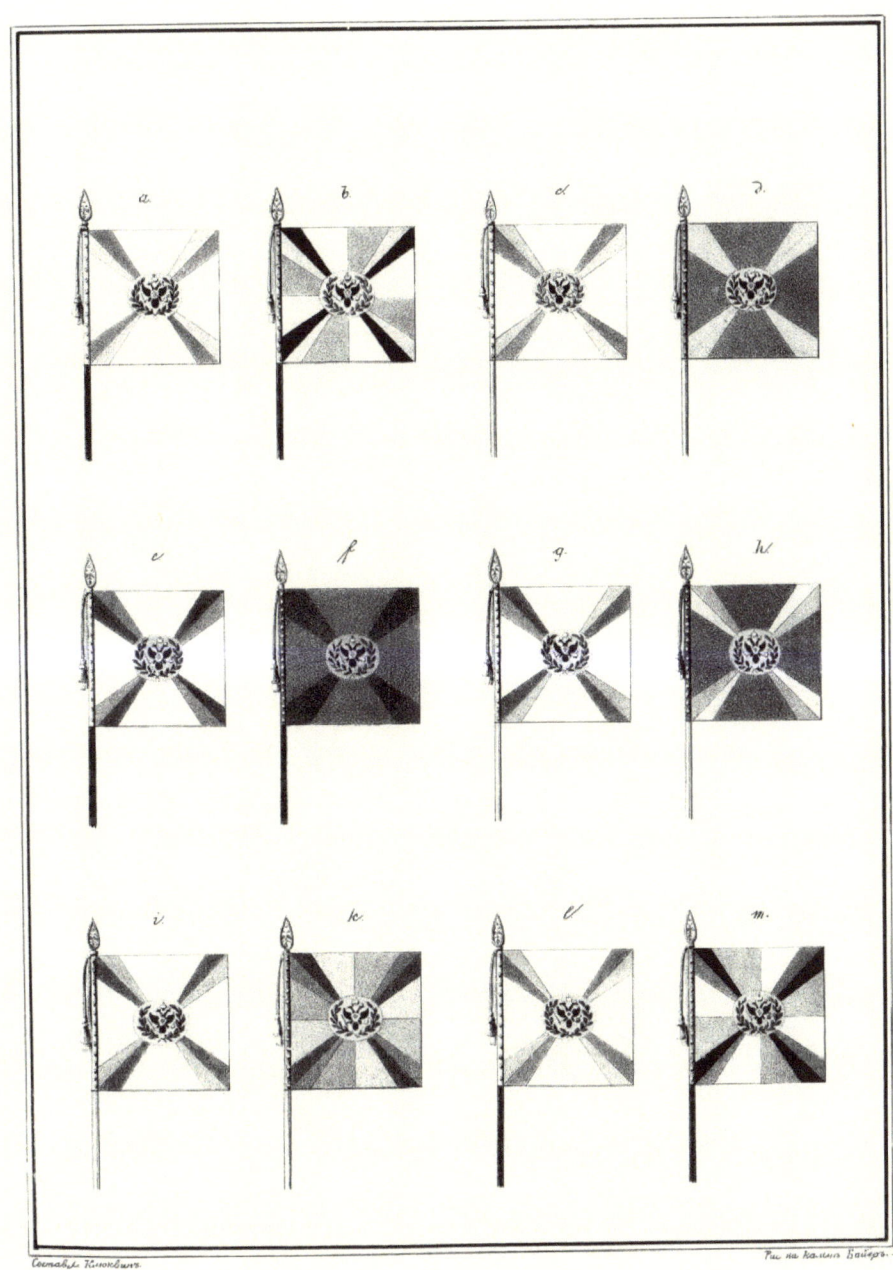

Flags granted to Garrison regiments: a-b. Staryi-Bykhov, 1799; c-d. Tomsk, 1799; e-f. Semi-palatinsk, 1799; g-h. Biisk, 1799; i-k. Petropavlovsk, 1799; l-m. Mozdok, 1799.

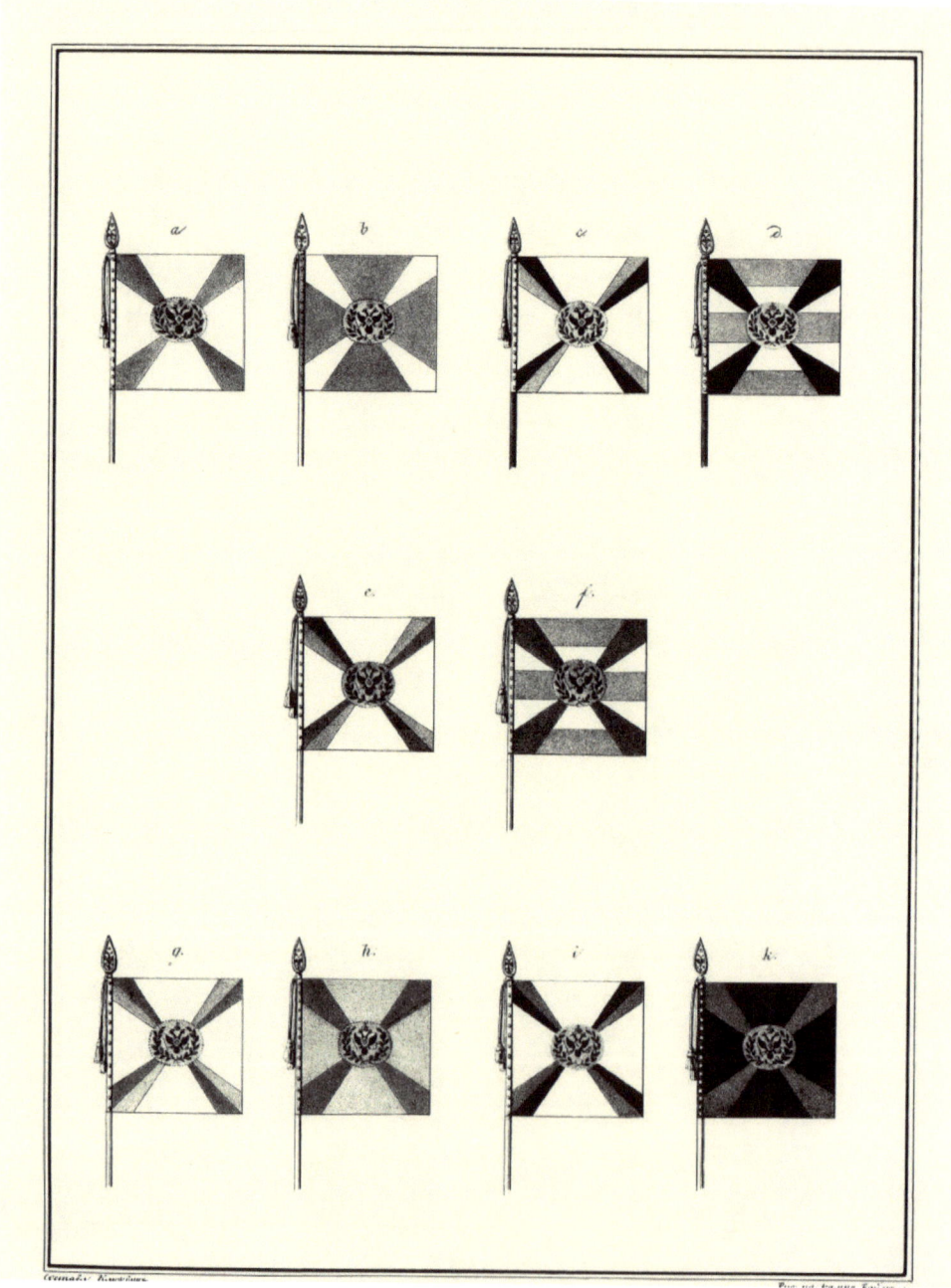

Flags granted to Garrison regiments: a-b. Saratov, 1798; c-d. Rochensalm, 1798; e-f. Sevasto-pol, 1798; g-h. Nikolaev, 1798; i-k. Niznhii-Kamchatka, 1799.

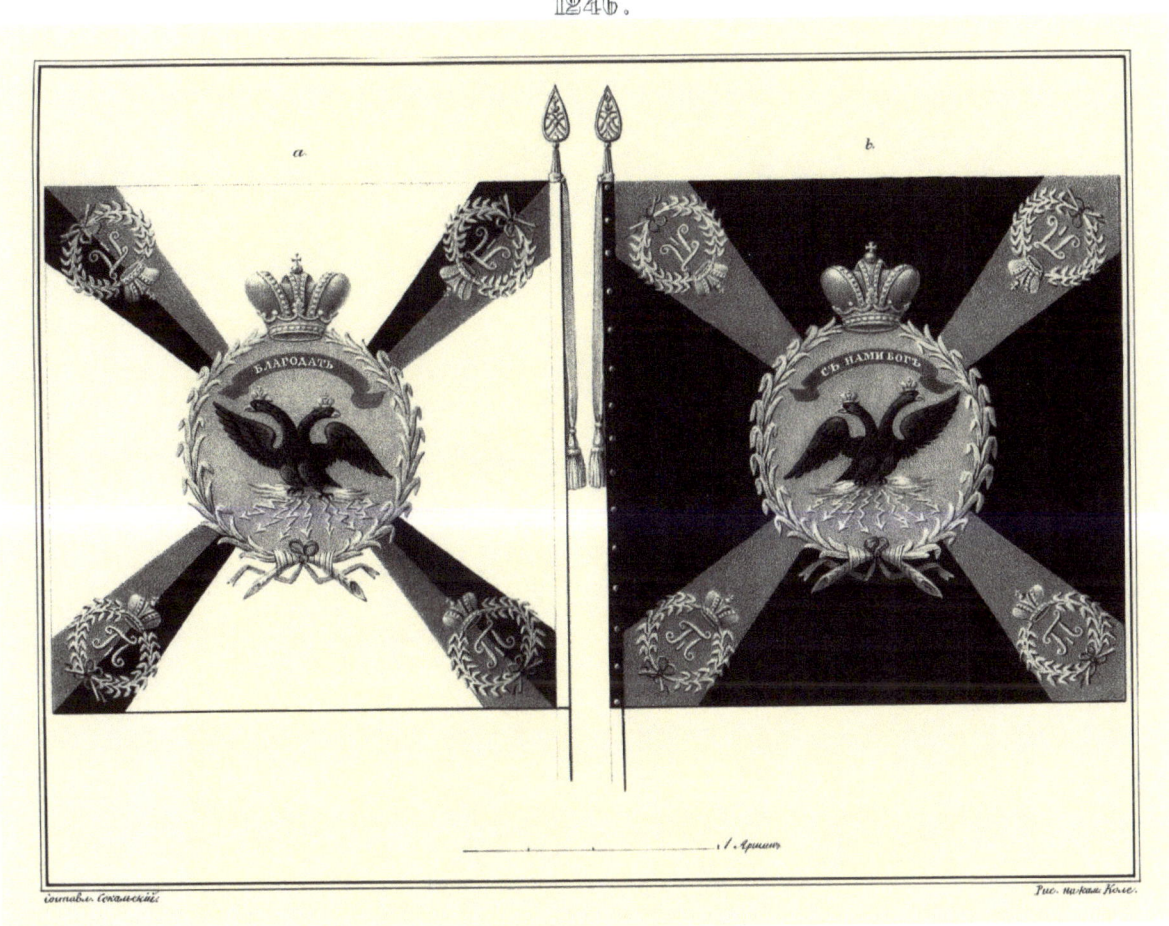

Flags established in 1800 for Army and Garrison regiments of the Lifland, Lithuania, Smolensk, and Brest Inspectorates.

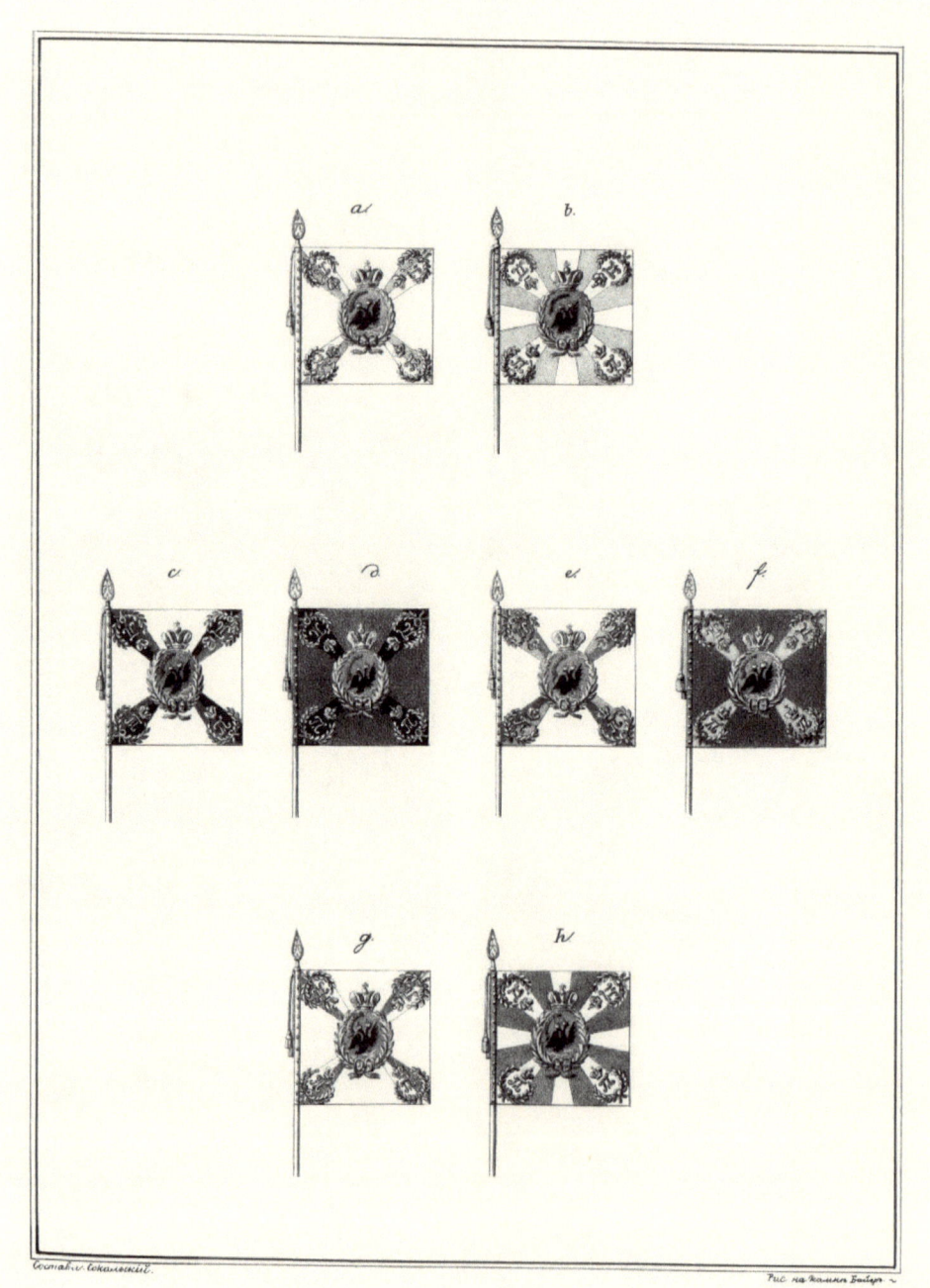

Flags established in 1800 for Army and Garrison regiments: a-b. Regiments of the Ukraine, Dniester, Crimea, and Caucasus Inspectorates; c-d. Finland Inspectorate; e-f. Orenburg and Siberia Inspectorates; g-h. St.-Peterburg and Moscow Inspectorates.

Flag granted to the Taurica Grenadier Regiment, 30 March 1800

Standards granted to His Majesty's Leib-Cuirassier Regiment, 25 June 1798.

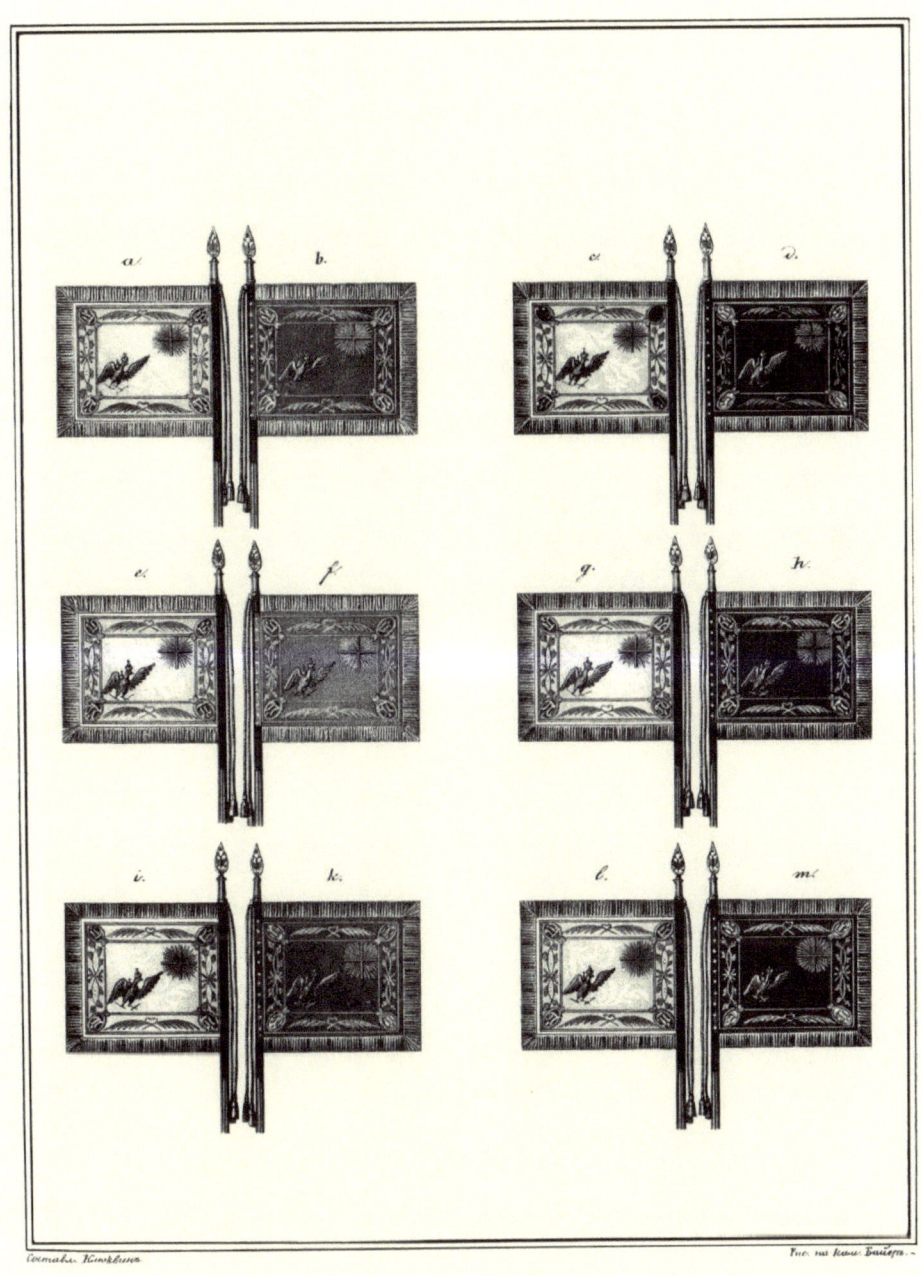

1250.

Standards granted to Cuirassier regiments: a-b. Her Majesty's, 1798; c-d. Military Order, 1798; e-f. Yekaterinoslav, 1798; g-h. Kazan, 1798; i-k. Ryazan, 1798; l-m. Yamburg, 1798.

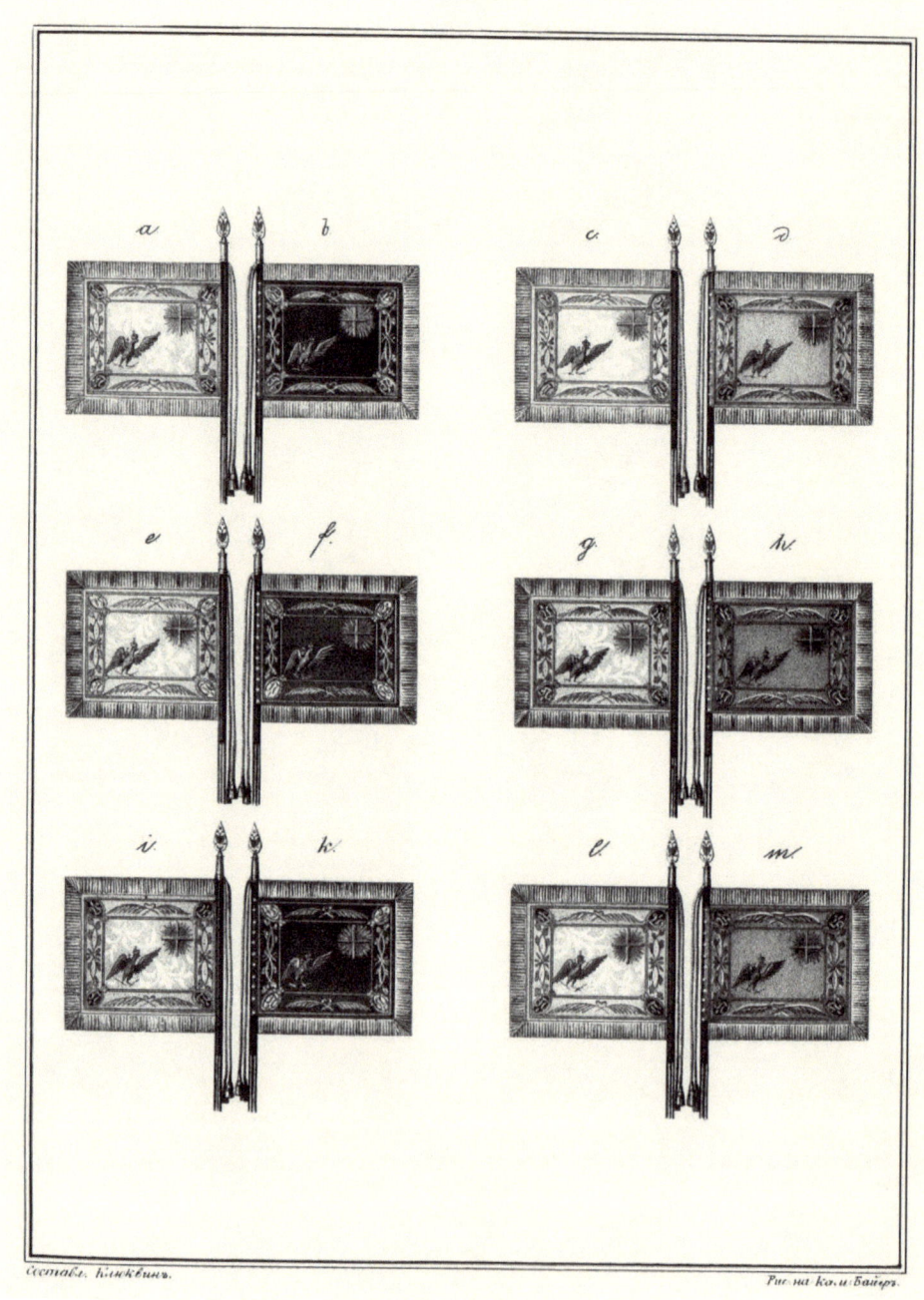

Standards granted to Cuirassier regiments: a-b. Glukhov, 1798; c-d. Kiev, 1798; e-f. Nezhin, 1798; g-h. Sofiya, 1798; i-k. Starodub, 1798; l-m. Chernigov, 1798.

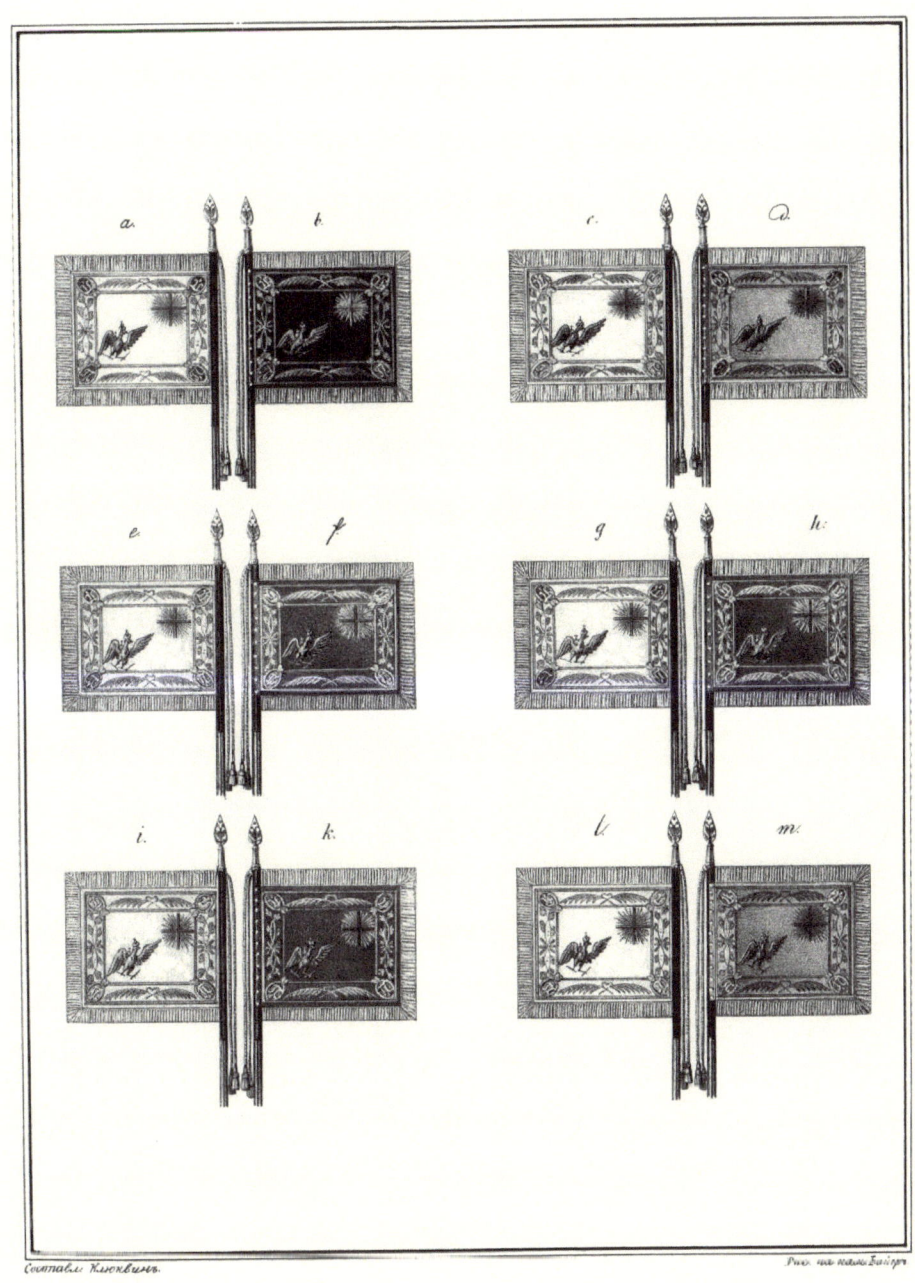

Standards granted to Cuirassier regiments: a-b. Riga, 1798; c-d. Kharkov, 1798; e-f. Little Russia, 1798; g-h. Friderici's, 1799; i-k. Neplyuev's, 1798; l-m. Zorn's, 1799.

1253.

Standards granted to the Vladimir Dragoon Regiment, 21 January 1799.

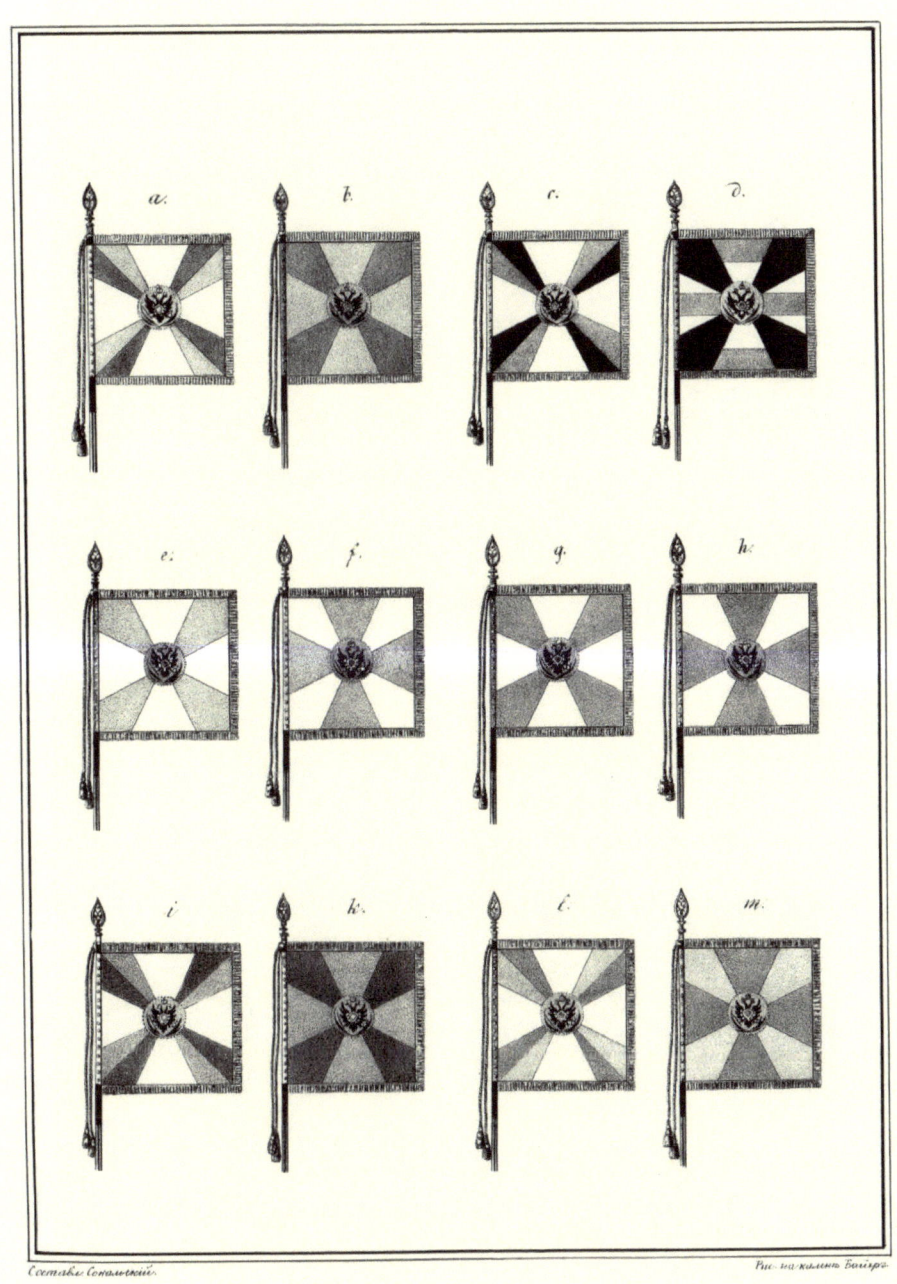

Standards granted to Dragoon regiments: a-b. Astrakhan, 1797; c-d. Nizhnii-Novgorod, 1799; e-f. Pskov, 1798; g-h. St. Petersburg, 1798; i-k. Smolensk, 1798; l-m. Taganrog, 1799.

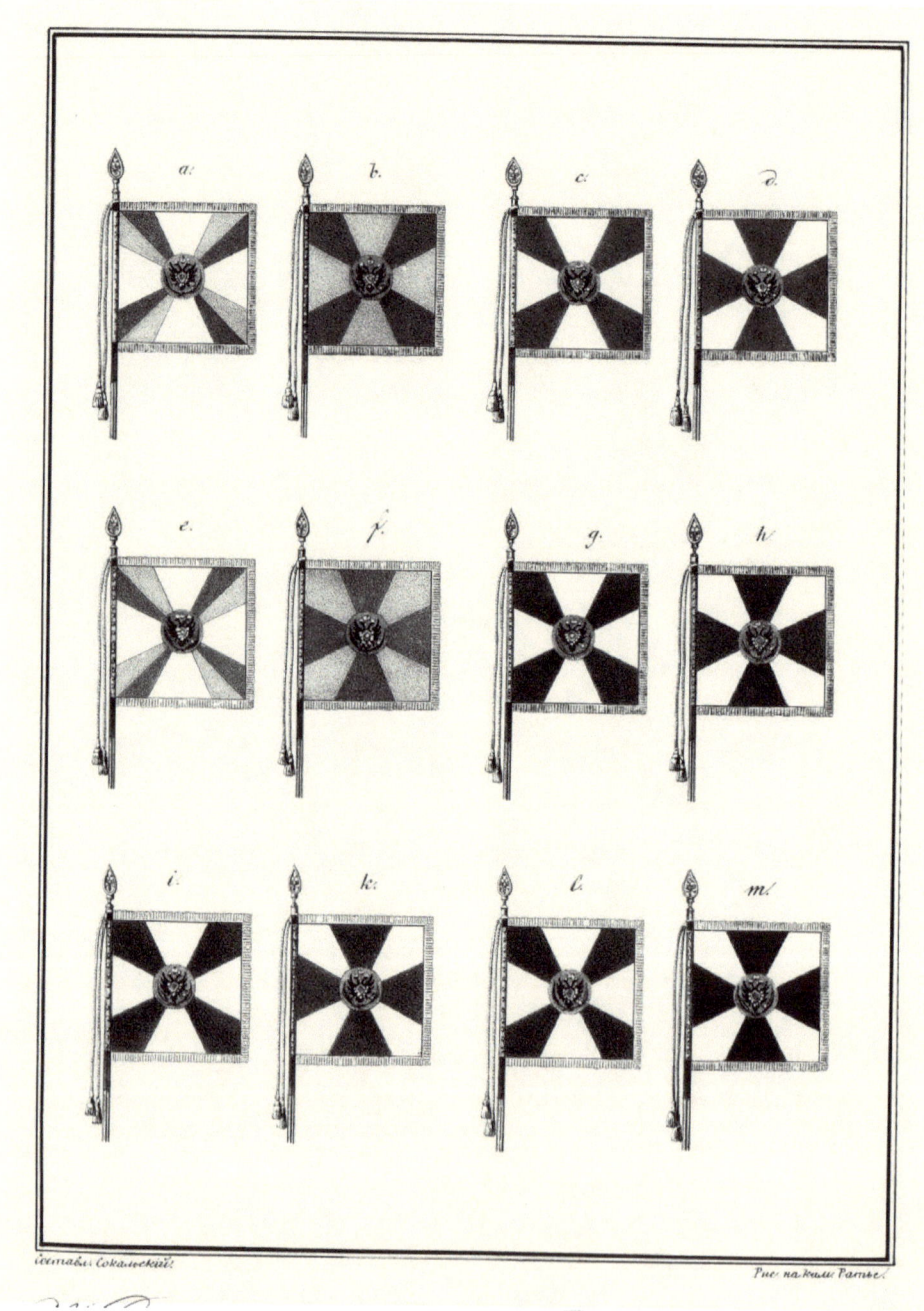

Standards granted to Dragoon regiments: a-b. Irkutsk, 1797; c-d. Orenburg, 1797; e-f. Siberia, 1797; g-h. Ingermanland, 1798; i-k. Narva, 1799; l-m. Rostov, 1798.

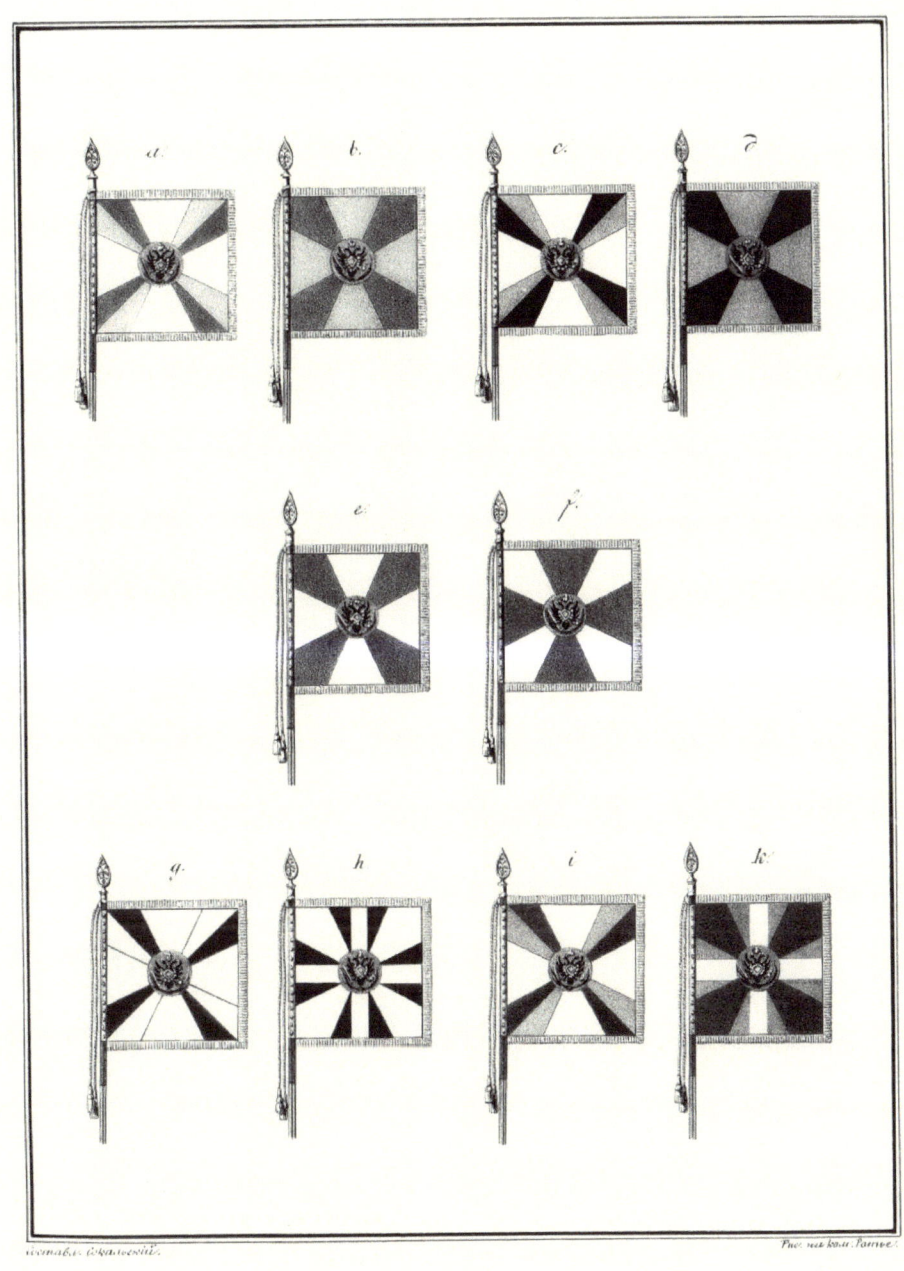

Standards granted to Dragoon regiments: a-b. Moscow, 1798; c-d. Seversk, 1798; e-f. Kargopol, 1798; g-h. Schreider's, 1799; i-k. Khastatov's, 1799.

1257.

Standards granted in 1800 to the Dragoon Regiments of Skalon, Pushkin, and Obrezkov.

Flags granted to Life-Guards regiments in December 1796. a. Preobrazhenskii, b. Semenovskii, c. Iz-
mailovskii. Note: These flags were granted without Maltese crosses, which were sewn on later, in 1798.

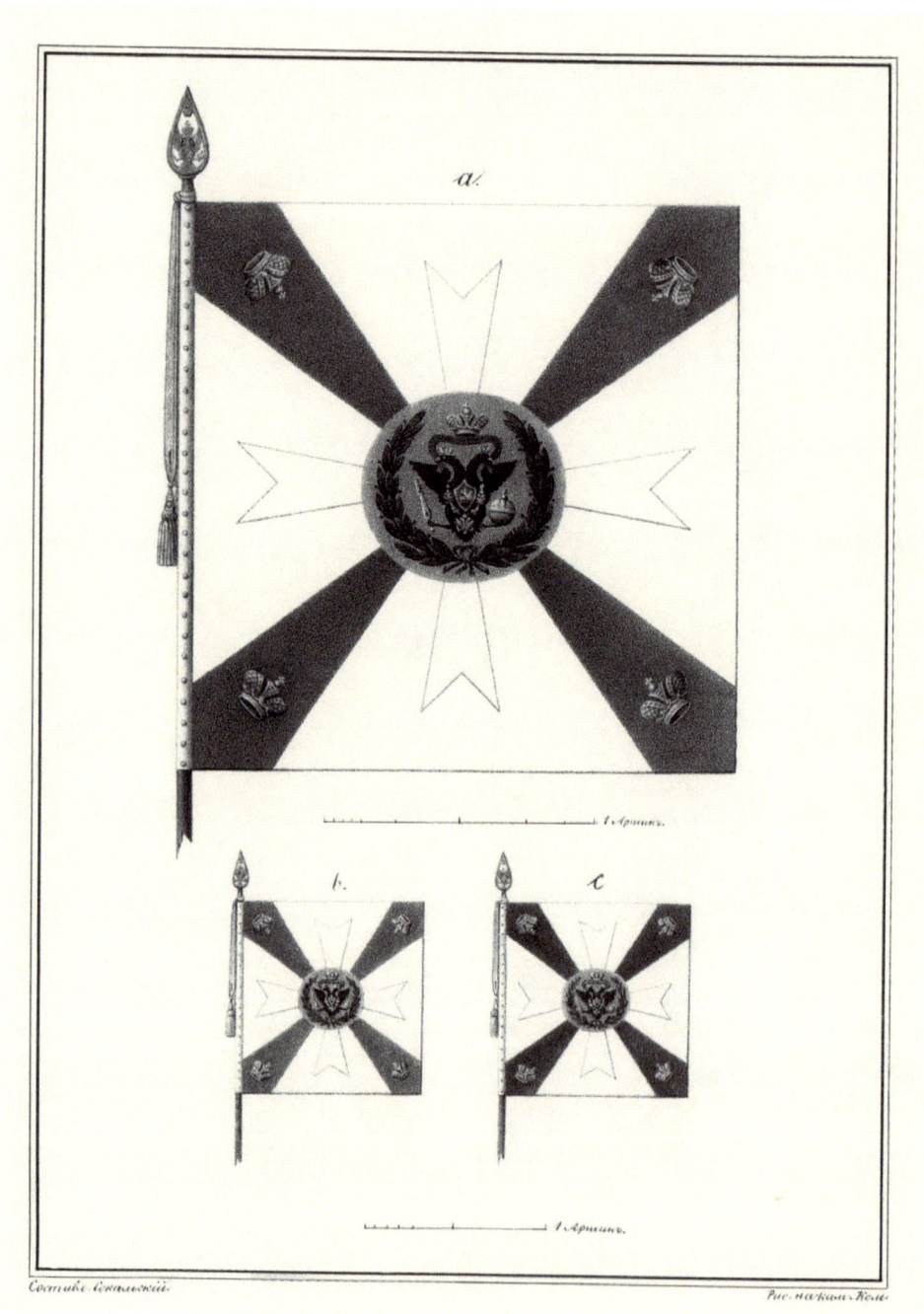

Flags granted to Chef battalions in the Life Guards, 2 January 1798. a. Preobrazhenskii, b. Semenovskii, c. Izmailovskii.

Flags granted to Chef battalions in the Life Guards, 2 January 1798. a. Preobrazhenskii, b. Semenovskii, c. Izmailovskii.

Flags granted to Life-Guards regiments, 7 January 1799. a. Preobrazhenskii, b. Semenovskii, c. Izmailovskii.

Flags granted to Life-Guards regiments, 7 January 1799. a. Preobrazhenskii, b. Semenovskii, c. Izmailovskii.

Flags intended for the Life-Guards Preobrazhenskii, Semenovskii, and Izmailovskii Regiments, 1800. below: Cavalier-Guards Standards. a. Cavalier Guards Corps, granted in 1799; b. Cavalier Guards Regiment, granted in 1800; c. Cavalier Guards Regiment, granted in 1800.

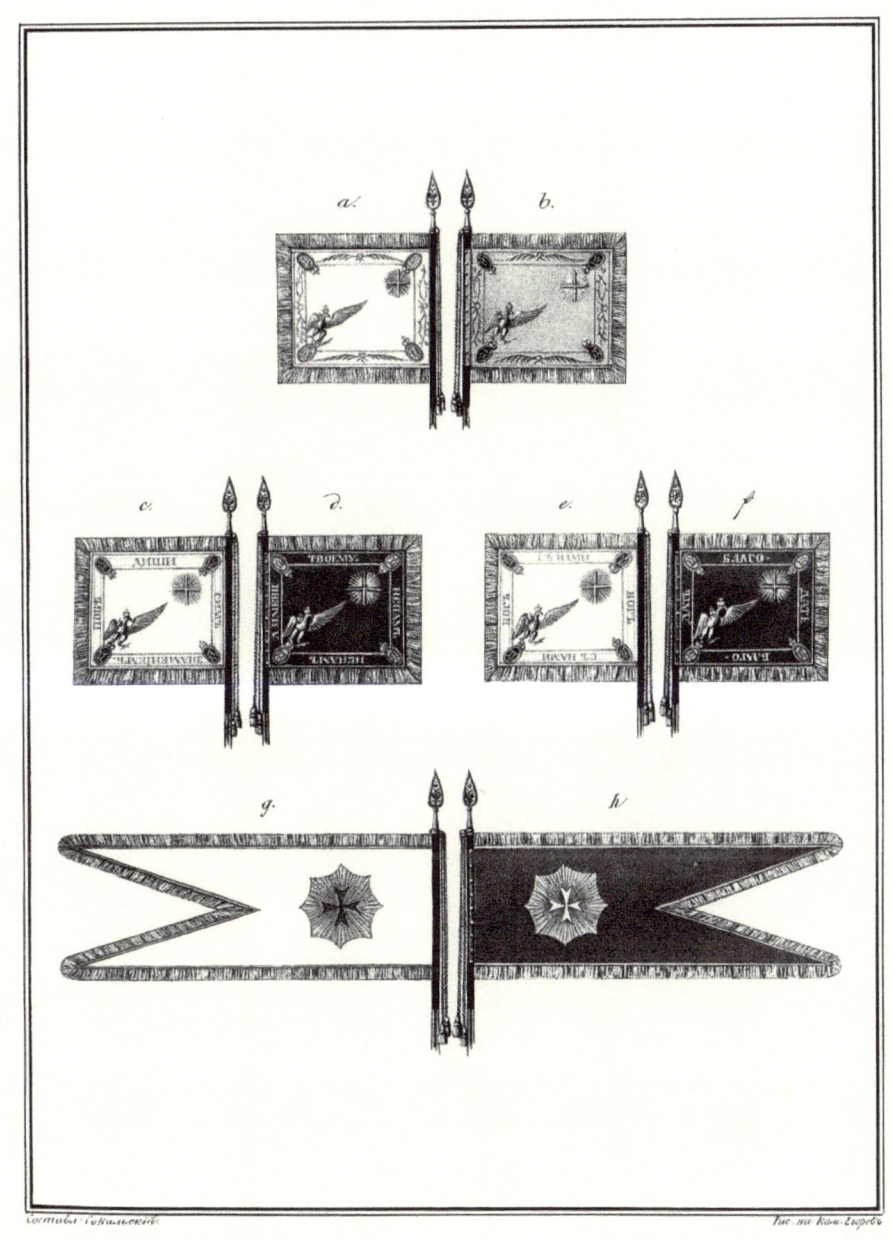

Standards granted to Life-Guards regiments: a-b. Horse, 1796; c-d. Horse, 1798; e-f. Horse, 1799; g-h. Cossack, 1799.

1266.

Flags granted to the Army (later 1st) Cadet Corps, 2 November 1798.

Flag granted to the Ural Host, 19 April 1798.

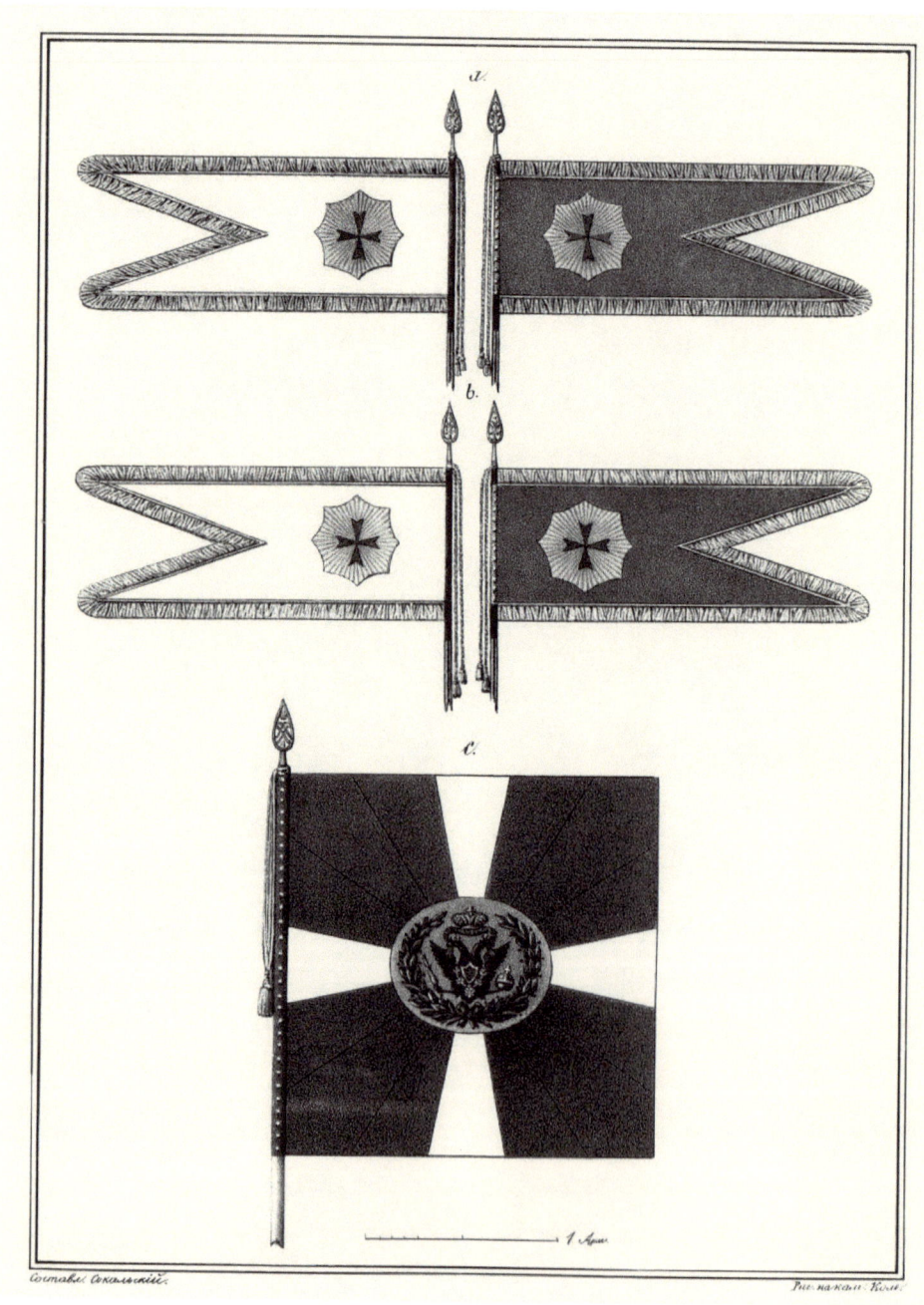

Flags granted to Cossack troops: a. 1st Chuguev Regiment, 10 August 1798; b. 2nd Chuguev Regiment, 10 August 1798; c. Leib-Ural Sotnia, 4 January 1799.

Flag granted to the Don Host, 15 February 1800.

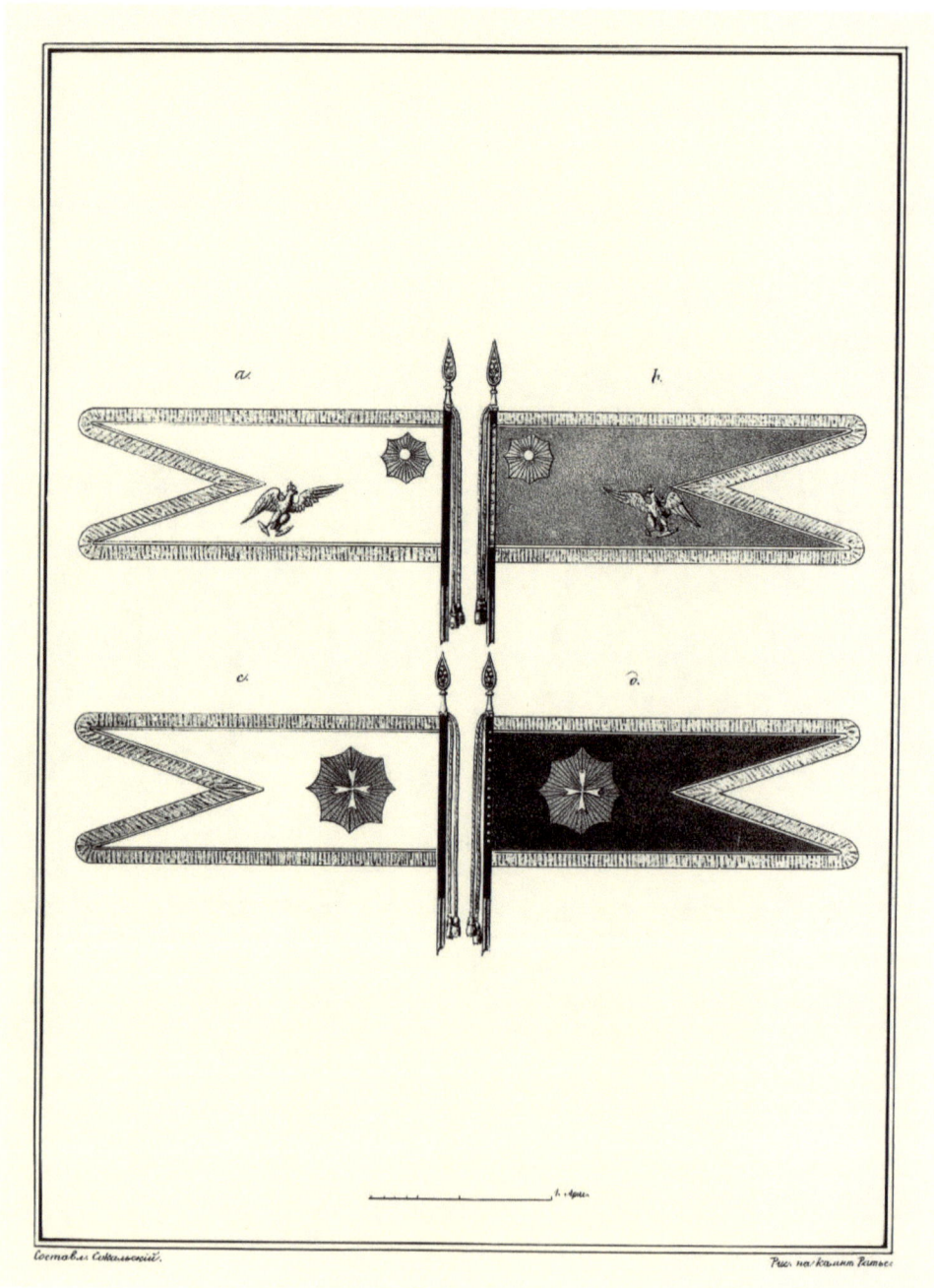

Flags granted to Horse regiments, 15 September 1798: a-b. Lithuanian, Tatar; c-d. Polish.

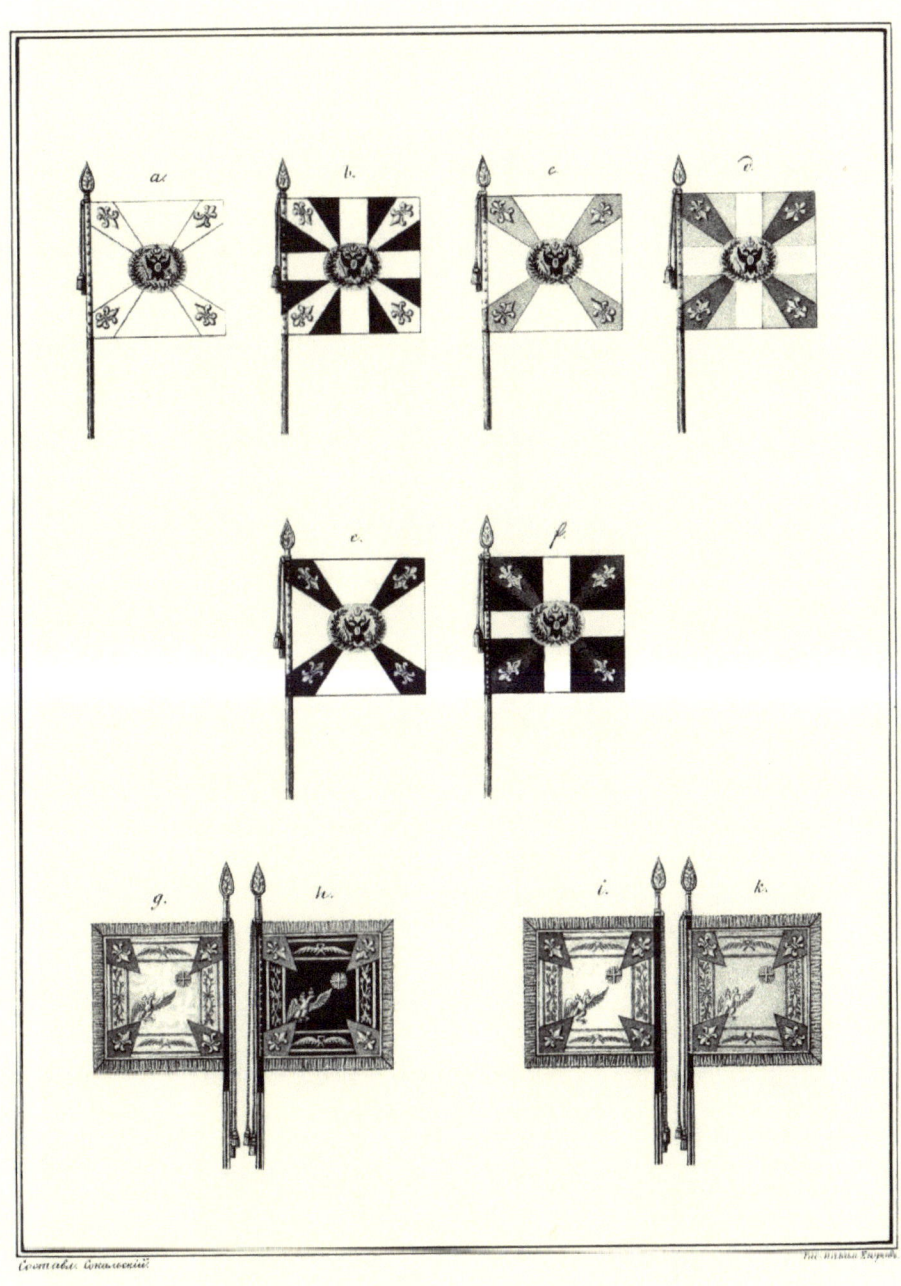

Flags and standards granted to reg. in the Prince de Condé's Corps, 15 January 1798: a-b. Prince de Condé's French Noble Regiment; c-d. Duke de Bourbon's Grenadier Regiment; e-f. Duke de Hohenlohe's German Regiment; g-h. Duke de Berry's Noble Dragoon Reg. i-k. Duke d'Enghien's Dragoon Reg.

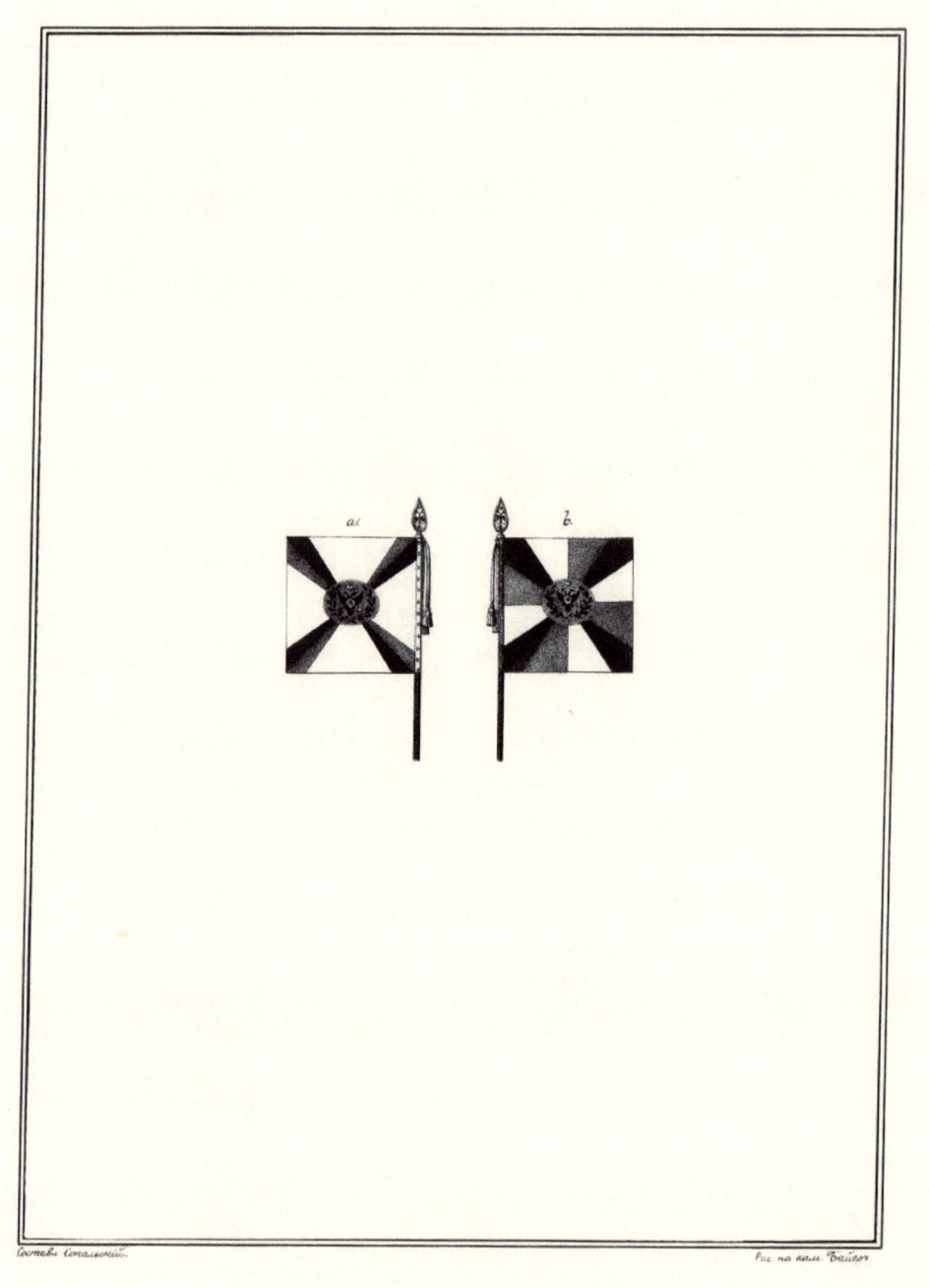

Flags granted to the Senate Battalion in 1799.

Medals instituted for award to lower military ranks for twenty years' service without reproach.
a. St. Anne, 12 November 1796; b. Donative of St. John of Jerusalem, 10 October 180

WORK PLAN

Our reprint in based on the original 19th century volumes, to be precise the volumes from 7 to 9 are dedicated to the reign of Paul I; this first part is distributed on 7 volumes, having a numbering from 1 to 7. From number 10 to 18 of the original volumes, the second part is dedicated to the Russian troops under Alexander I. These still being worked on and they will be soon ready, distributed on twenty volumes approximately. Our new edition, the first ever published in English, both on paper and digital format, boasts a large number of color plates, many of them unpublished and coloured by our team of expert artists and scholars of uniformology. Each volume is based on 50/70 plates, always accompanied by the original translated text which describes the uniforms, the organization and the armament of the Russian army of the period.

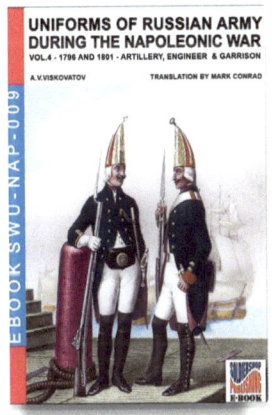

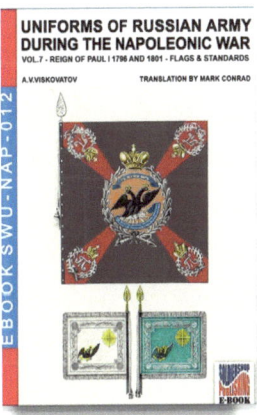